P9-BIM-770

BOOKS BY DARYL HINE

POETRY

Academic Festival Overtures   1985
Selected Poems   1981
Daylight Saving   1978
Resident Alien   1975
In and Out   1975
Minutes   1968
The Wooden Horse   1965
The Devil's Picture Book   1961
The Carnal and the Crane   1957
Five Poems   1954

FICTION

The Prince of Darkness and Co.   1961

TRAVEL

Polish Subtitles   1962

TRANSLATION

Theocritus: Idylls and Epigrams   1982
The Homeric Hymns AND
The Battle of the Frogs and the Mice   1972

ACADEMIC
FESTIVAL
OVERTURES

DARYL HINE

ACADEMIC FESTIVAL OVERTURES

ATHENEUM
NEW YORK
1985

Library of Congress Cataloging-in-Publication Data

Hine, Daryl.
    Academic festival overtures.

    1. Holidays—Poetry. I. Title.
PR9199.3.H5A67 1985   811'.54   84–45704
ISBN 0–689–11573–3
ISBN 0–689–11580–6 (pbk.)

FOR GÉRARD CASPARY

Gaudeamus igitur, juvenes dum sumus.

CONTENTS

ACADEMIC
FESTIVAL
OVERTURES

SEPTEMBER: LABOUR DAY

For me, as for anyone who was educated
    In the same system, the year has always begun
In effect with the first day of school in September,
    Not, like the calendar, on January One.
The annual renewal of the Winter Solstice
    Has been observed at the Autumnal Equinox
For generations among schoolchildren, whose habits
    Are strictly regulated like their body clocks
By an arbitrary institutional rhythm
    That dictates their daily lives propaideutically
From the commencement exercise of kindergarten
    To the conferral of the terminal degree,
Which time will award even to failures and drop-outs,
    An existential, honorary Q.E.D.
Further, for those who have eccentrically elected
    To remain in the educational domain,
Until their dismissal or superannuation
    The opening of school looms again and again,
Not as in that recurrent academic nightmare
    Of an exam for which one is poorly prepared,
But with a dull anticipatory excitement
    If anything heightened by being slightly scared,
As before a debut or an initiation
    One wonders what wisdom experience may bring,
And if the tentative arrangements scored in Autumn
    Will still be played as harmoniously come Spring?
For the return to class functions like a rehearsal
    As the annual silly symphony recurs
And in the pit the unpractised juvenile players
    Strike up academic festival overtures.

He sat a seat ahead of me beside the window
    Which was wide open, across the aisle in home room,
1949, the first day of Junior High School,
    And, half turning, smiled ambiguously—at whom?

I had to wait to find out his name till the teacher
    We called the Mackerel, alias Miss MacColl,
After *O Canada*, The Lord's Prayer, and a reading
    From the Bible, took alphabetical roll-call,
To which we one by one foolishly answered "Present,"
    As ignorant of the future as of the past.
After Tim Soderstrom, Alf Stevens and John Thomas,
    His long-awaited name, Donald Wisdom, came last,
Whereat he impertinently responded, "Absent,"
    Which got a big laugh from the class and a severe
Look from the teacher. He created the impression
    Of being beautifully anywhere but here,
Although possessed of an undeniable presence
    In the flesh, with his fresh, exceptional good looks.

I could not take my eyes from his new-minted profile
    While we were instructed where to open our books
For our first lesson. The study of English grammar
    Was one in which as a rule I easily shone,
But I resolved to hide that light under a bushel
    And sat on my hands when I saw Don Wisdom yawn.
Anyway, how can an image of such perfection
    Be adumbrated by an adjective or noun?
What figure of speech would be adequate to capture
    The curve of a cheek faintly embellished with down,
The nape of a neck framed by what might have been ringlets
    Had his blond locks not been militarily clipped
In the fashion of the forties, regular features
    Composing a strange face, blue-eyed, straight-nosed, full-lipped.
There were other boys—and girls—in the class as handsome—
    Or as pretty—some slightly more so, I suppose:
At that age physical charm is not that uncommon.
    But rivalled, here by an eyebrow, there by a nose,
He had the dynamic yet unconscious attraction
    Not of a statue but an athlete in repose.

The book in my lap (I had the habit of reading
    Surreptitiously in class) described to a T
His commonplace, immature but heart-breaking beauty,

Or rather its title did: *Fearful Symmetry.*
(Its contents were a pioneering commentary
    On the poet, painter and prophet William Blake
Whom I preferred to his classic contemporary,
    The set author of the dull *Lady of the Lake.*)
Inattentive to the unnecessary lesson—
    Had I not taught myself as a toddler to read?
Grateful for tutelage in French and mathematics,
    Of literary instruction I felt no need—
My eyes also strayed from my alternative reading
    To study Wisdom's averted face like a book
In some incomprehensible yet cognate language,
    Provoking an oblique, interrogative look.
But when suddenly I was irritably summoned
    To diagram a complex sentence on the board,
And did so with affected insolence, correctly,
    My audience merely continued to look bored.
This was considered the appropriate expression
    In class—not, I admit, without sufficient cause;
While I often yawned myself, I was stimulated
    By the discrete charm of a subordinate clause.
For me grammar had an indisputable glamour
    With its elastic yet indispensable laws;
But to most children the educational system
    Was like a bankrupt, empty-handed Santa Claus.
Had anyone informed them that syntax is sexist,
    As to some radical feminists it appears,
In the sense that the subject dominates the object,
    Possibly that would have made them prick up their ears,
In the case of most boys protruberant already
    From short hair. Colloquially untroubled by
Finicky distinctions of person, case and number,
    They persist in cheerfully saying *lay* for *lie.*
Formal grammar was not descriptive but prescriptive
    In those days, at least at Lord Lovat Junior High
Where many a proscribed vernacular locution
    Freely bandied about in whispers in the halls
Although blameless was tainted by association
    With the enormities inscribed on washroom walls,

Words and phrases to be found in no dictionary
        We knew of, plain if disreputable speech,
A despised but strong alternative oral tradition
        It was thought improper, and redundant, to teach,
Including innocent but infra dig. expressions
        Such as the description of a child as a kid,
As well as other, less innocuous constructions
        Which girls were not supposed to understand, but did.
Certain terms, incorrectly called double entendres,
        Used casually, caused the knowing to explode
In sniggers, giving initiates the illusion,
        Dear to all conspirators, of cracking a code.
Ordinary discourse is strewn with many pitfalls
        The prudent and the prudish pretend to ignore
At their peril, many a matter-of-fact statement
        Concealing an undesirable metaphor.
Most adults seemed genuinely to have forgotten
        Quite the lore and language of schoolchildren, along
With childhood itself, hence their repressive assumption
        That anything children said or did must be wrong.
So grammar became an instrument of oppression,
        Or if you prefer of a radical reform,
Replacing the natural anarchy of the playground
        With the classroom's deceptive artificial norm,
To which I subscribed with naive enthusiasm,
        Seeing in its aesthetic and logical shape
A way out of my painful, pubescent confusion,
        A cast-iron, intellectual fire escape.

I regained my seat, having completed my sentence
        In a silence more eloquent than any praise;
Without comment Miss MacColl continued the lesson
        Until in the midst of an adjectival phrase
A buzzer interrupted the unfinished structure
        Of her instruction, and she laid aside her chalk
With a sigh as we stirred from our studious stupour.
        "It is not a fire drill, children. Don't run, but walk,"
Unable to stop the stampede into the hallway
        Of giddily giggling girls and boisterous boys.

This brief transition between classes embodied
    Pandemonium: the confusion, and the noise!
Not that all of us were the dirty little devils
    That so many of our preceptors seemed to think,
With our new, best clothes, clean fingernails and scrubbed faces
    Immaculate enough but for acne and ink.
I must add to complete the traditional picture
    Of hell an overwhelming, not unhealthy stink
Of hot and hyperactive adolescent bodies
    Compounded of tobacco, brilliantine and sweat.
There was just enough time—five minutes—between classes
    To sneak into the washroom for a cigarette,
A vice which, along with certain other bad habits,
    I had either given up or not acquired yet,
And a den of vice I hesitated to enter,
    With its smoky atmosphere and smoking-room talk.
Instead I stood stupidly in front of my locker
    Fiddling futilely with its combination lock.
As I was doing so somebody jogged my elbow
    In passing, causing me to drop my loose-leaf book;
When I bent to pick it up I saw Donald Wisdom
    Going on without a smile, a word, or a look;
Yet his gesture constituted a recognition
    Of sorts, itself a source of indefinite hope,
As he left in his wake a wave of speculation
    As well as the heady scent of Ivory soap.
I followed him indiscreetly but at a distance
    With the devotion of an undercover cop
Through the hectic hall and down the stairs to the basement
    And our next class, vocational training, or shop.
Here the sexes, but not the classes, separated,
    The females to pleonastically named Home Ec.,
Males to metalwork, woodwork, mechanical drawing,
    Subjects which most would major in later at Tech.,
When classmates would be invidiously divided
    According to aptitude, those who had good grades
Going to academic high school to learn Latin,
    The others elsewhere to study practical trades.
But for the time being undifferentiated

Students plainly destined for such different schools
In Junior High were willy-nilly all subjected
      To the same first lesson, "Taking care of our tools".
This could hardly fail to raise a tumescent titter
      In pubescent circles, which did not seem to vex
Mr. Manley, our imperturbable instructor
      Who also taught Personal Hygiene, i.e. Sex
Ed., like woodwork considered a masculine province,
      While girls who one would have thought had much more to lose
By ignorance, were kept in the dark on the topic
      Of prophylaxis as well as vices and screws.
No wonder that so many of them became pregnant
      And never learned properly how to change a fuse.
For that matter, our own information was sketchy
      At that age; apart from some loose talk about loose
Women, most official disinformation treated
      The imaginary drawbacks of self-abuse.

My uncommon aversion to Manual Training
      At the time I superficially understood
As something at the same time sexual and snobbish,
      A disinclination for what I was no good
At, liking the inflexibility of metal
      Much less than the knotty vitality of wood.
This material, in which our province abounded,
      While not as forbidding as unforgiving steel,
I infinitely preferred in the form of paper—
      A preference my handy classmates did not feel,
For whom shop was a proper form of self-expression
      And handicrafts a hobby instead of a chore,
Almost as much fun as physical education
      Which I also considered a bore, all the more
So in view of the normal high-spirited horseplay
      And ostentatiously masculine atmosphere
Which I resented as indecently suggestive:
      Though different, I did not yet know I was queer.
Practices that I condemned as childish and selfish
      For some months now I had firmly put on the shelf

Where they constituted an on-going temptation
    I strenuously and daily denied myself.

While my classmates larked about their lathes and work-benches
    I stood stolidly staring in disgust at mine
On which our first assignment was to manufacture
    A cylindrical object of pointless design.
To an imagination enflamed by repression
    Innocent things appear in a sinister light;
But if the others noticed any rude resemblance
    They exploited it in a manner to excite
Collusive laughter. I slyly observed Don Wisdom
    Plying his chisel with ambiguous delight,
Partly with an affected salacious enjoyment
    And in part with the will to get the job done right.
Here incompetence and shyness made me an outsider
    To a degree that I was not in English class;
But if these fifty minutes seemed practically endless
    Even an eternity of boredom must pass.

With incredulous relief I greeted the signal
    That freed me from the thrall of my detested bench
As it summoned the reluctant to their next lesson,
    Which, this being Tuesday and Canada, was French,
Imperatively but imperfectly imparted
    By an old maid said to have once done time in France
Whose authentic but incomprehensible accent
    Encouraged our incorrigible ignorance.
The problem with French being its pronunciation
    By the untutored, clumsy, English-speaking tongue,
It presented almost insurmountable pitfalls
    To the tongue-tied, often monosyllabic young.
Another peculiar feature of French, gender—
    A sensitive topic at our age to begin
With—puzzled us with its irrational division
    Of the world into masculine and feminine.
This left-over of a primitive animism
    Scandalized our undifferentiated sense

Of things, as did in an opposite sense the absence
    In French of all regular syllabic accénts.
Those foreign accents, grave, acute and circumflexive,
    Seemed inessential, ornamental, and absurd
As a cedilla, yet their timely imposition
    Could Frenchify the most homely domestic word.
In short the language of diplomacy was treated
    By my young countrymen as a dubious joke;
Evidemment, Donald Wisdom was no exception
    To the widespread distrust of all things alien,
Which most of our countrymen consider hardly human:
    But what did we know of alienation then?
Par exemple, questioned in turn how he was going
    Or how he carried himself, by Mademoiselle,
He answered with a shrug that might have passed for Gallic
    Which the teacher interpreted as, Very well,
But of which the rest of us recognized the meaning
    To be something more impolite, like Go to hell.
Soon tired, myself, as so often, of conversation,
    I pondered the paradigms in the grammar book.
Kitchen French may be all very well in the kitchen:
    I had no intention, then, of being a cook.
While it would be an emphatic exaggeration
    To claim that the only good language is a dead
One, as in the case of classical Greek and Latin,
    Tongues were, for me, primarily meant to be read.
When presently I graduated from the precious
    Child's play of Perrault to the chilled plays of Racine,
Strange how at once I speechlessly appreciated
    The rigorous longeurs of the Alexandrine.
Such a facility for languages is suspect
    Among those with a shaky command of their own;
Even in our officially bilingual nation
    Few Canadians are fluently allophone.
In keeping my bilingualism a secret,
    As others conceal their bisexuality,
I found such discretion greatly facilitated
    By a lack of practical opportunity.
But for the present, the imperfect and the future,

Booby traps in the *dictées* that Mademoiselle
Sprung on us daily, were blithely obliterated
    By the long-awaited sound of the noontime bell,
Spelling the end of another round of the prize fight
    And instantaneously liberating us
Who had outgrown the grade-school midmorning recess
    For lunch hour, like some shrill secular angelus.

The halls quickly filled with and more quickly emptied
    Of a headlong, migratory, ravening herd
That stampeded towards freedom outside the exits,
    All recalls to order unheeded or unheard.
The fortunate went home for lunch, which some called dinner,
    As I had always done till this unhappy day;
Since my mother's terminal hospitalization
    I did not have much home to go to anyway.
Before he went to work in the morning my worried
    Father, an elementary school principal,
Had bagged my lunch, a roast beef sandwish and an apple.
    Grasping this in hand, I entered the hospital
Ward the landscape had become in early September
    Where nature lay dying, neglected and in pain,
Under an oxygen tent of diluted sunshine
    Made precious by the ever-present threat of rain.
Opposite the school an uncultivated public
    Park provided a kind of privacy for those,
Like lovers and loners, who wanted it, a playground
    For the energetic, and a place of repose
For the lazy. Myself an indifferent athlete,
    Looking forward with mixed apprehension to gym,
I glanced in passing at a bunch of soccer players
    In the midst of whom I thought I recognized him
Whom my eyes desired the sight of above all others,
    In a green argyle sweater and cream corduroys,
But I saw on second look that I was mistaken,
    For it was only another one of the boys.
Disappointed, I opened my unappetizing
    Picnic lunch in a virgin stand of Douglas firs,
The evergreen emblem of a lumbering province

Rich in such grandiose but gloomy conifers,
Turning the pages of my book with greasy fingers
    Slick with mayonnaise, meantime devouring as well
Frye's digest of that indigestible farrago
    Of paradox, The Marriage of Heaven & Hell.
Omnivorous youth! indiscriminately gorging
    On the soggy sandwich and the indignant page
With an appetite at once healthy and voracious,
    Unlike the fussy gourmandise of middle age.
Undisturbed by the distant sound of striving voices,
    For the first time that morning I forgot the time,
Absorbed in the similarities of an era
    When, as nowadays, love sweet love was thought a crime,
Or at the very least a childish peccadillo,
    Something mother would not consider very nice,
Under the shadow of whose moribund injunctions
    Reading had become my sole solitary vice,
In the course of which I had come across some puzzling
    References to the mores of ancient Greece
The tone of which reinforced La Rochefoucauld's maxim,
    "Les plaisirs d'autrui, on les appelle des vices."
If there were anything vicious in my rare pleasures
    I did not suspect it: ignoring Blake's advice,
I not only nursed desires unacted but posted
    No Trespassing over the gates of paradise.

My lunch hours would not always be so solitary
    And studious, as I made, not exactly friends,
But the kind of superficial, nodding acquaintance
    On which casual sociability depends;
Yet the most intellectually stimulating
    Interval in an otherwise somewhat humdrum
Day remained lunch: I learned from independent study
    Much more than from the regular curriculum.
At that epoch no special education classes
    Existed, at least to my knowledge, in B.C.,
For the retarded, the handicapped, or the gifted,
    Any of which sub-groups might have included me,
As I was socially backward, had to wear glasses,

And had an I.Q. tested at one-fifty-three.
Nor would my father let me be accelerated
    For vague, professional reasons, lest I lose touch
With my age group, whom I seldom associated
    With in or out of school anyway very much.
I should be academically ready for college
    In a year or two, but would be constrained to wait
Another five years impatiently for the dullest
    Of my contemporaries to matriculate,
At a cost, not only of much scholastic boredom—
    I was used to that—but of spiritual pride,
A contempt for what I called ordinary people
    Which only infatuation could override.

Alerted by the extracurricular silence,
    Too distant and preoccupied to hear the bell
Summoning one and all from mid-day dissipations,
    I jumped up guiltily shutting the Book of Thel.
The playing fields and the corridor were deserted.
    It was plain that I was not only late but last
Back in the classroom, where Don Wisdom near my vacant
    Seat smiled enigmatically as I slunk past,
While, shrugging as if to say, Better late than never,
    Miss MacColl indulgently watched me take my place,
Overlooking my tardiness since I was clever.
    Nonetheless I blushed, shamefaced, feeling in disgrace
With fortune and mens' eyes, puerile public opinion
    Being so invidiously prepared to blame
Such egregious examples of special treatment,
    More susceptible though I was to guilt than shame.
Teacher's Pet, most opprobrious of appellations
    In grade school, had been improved on among the boys
By more specific and scandalous allegations
    Commonly expressed by a rude, sibilant noise.
Miss MacColl taught mathematics as well as English,
    And now she proceeded to inscribe on the board
In place of a sentence a right-angled triangle,
    While the class contrived to look both baffled and bored.
The more rambunctious boys in the back row sat silent,

Seeing nothing in the theorem to induce
Mirth, and the girls ceased to look smugly disapproving,
    Detecting no mischief in the hypotenuse.
But I, who had found little interest in numbers
    Hitherto, left cold by simple arithmetic,
Quickly mesmerized by the magic spell of Euclid
    Watched the demonstration like a conjuring trick
Whose terminal flourish, *Quod erat demonstrandum,*
    Abbreviated to Q.E.D., I was quick
Like Latin, to get the hang of: thus mathematics
    Which I used to consider terminally dull,
Gave me a heady taste for mental acrobatics
    And the attractions of the ineluctable,
The way in which propositions, at first sight funny
    And far-fetched, patently preposterous,
Step by inevitable step are demonstrated
    As not only true but perfectly obvious.
In addition to its unexceptionableness
    It was the purity of plane geometry,
Perturbed as I was by obscure and impure yearnings,
    Doubtless that reassured and elevated me
Yet failed to entertain my less squeamish coevals:
    What disturbed and disgusted me delighted them
Who preferred the real world with all its imperfections
    To the Platonic beauty of a theorem.
Perhaps because he looked inattentive, Don Wisdom
    Was asked to stand up and elucidate a proof,
Which he did with a flourish like a smirking angel,
    As beautiful as an angle and as aloof,
Nonchalantly illustrating the desired figure
    As if mindful of the advice, Only connect,
Before retiring to his seat leaving the answer
    For all to see, two-dimensional and correct.
Like mine his performance was acknowledged in silence;
    Though I should have liked to clap, it just was not done.
Of course he would have been (and often was) applauded
    For sinking a basket or hitting a home run.
Geometry had the status of a hard science,

Unlike the impractical arts at which I starred,
So proficiency in it was granted a grudging
    Approval by those who admired anything hard.
In all likelihood my own open admiration
    Possessed its hardly conscious competitive side
Which I was, while wholly unprepared to admit it,
    Insufficiently disingenuous to hide.
But if mathematics furnished a glimpse of heaven,
    The class scheduled after the penultimate bell
Of the school day promised, at least in apprehension,
    A foretaste, to me unpalatable, of hell.

Compulsory physical education, coming
    Hard on the heels of the developing physique,
Superseded the anarchic pastimes of childhood:
    Marbles, tug-of-war, blind man's buff, tag, hide-and-seek,
With tediously regimented exercises
    And organized games with arbitrary and strange
Rules that I could never be bothered to remember,
    For which, what was more, we all were supposed to change,
We who had already changed or were quickly changing,
    For whom nudity had been normally taboo,
Now were told to undress in front of one another,
    Something I for one was most reluctant to do.
You might rightly expect that I should be excited
    At the sight of my secret idol in the nude,
But I was because of my puritan upbringing,
    Although privately prurient, a public prude.
Had I not once fled in hypocritical horror
    The swimming pool at the local Y.M.C.A.
Where a Grecian dress-code innocently encouraged
    What I alone regarded as shameless display?
Therefore I was as usual the last to enter
    The locker-room, that rowdy labyrinth chock full
Of boisterous team-mates beautifully cavorting
    Like uninhibited young minotaurs, part bull.
Unnoticed I partially undressed in a corner
    With decent haste donning cotton singlet and shorts,

And followed the others out to the bright palaestra,
    Onto the delineated basketball courts,
Like the courts of the temple of physical culture,
    Where the language spoken by all but me was Sports.
Those years in which the memory is most retentive
    Were, with few exceptions like mine, if I recall,
Wasted not in the paper chase of verbal learning,
    But in the frenetic pursuit of some dumb ball.

First on the floor face down we performed callisthenics,
    Which (I looked it up) meant Beauty Through Strength, in Greek,
Though I confess the aesthetic appeal of push-ups
    Appeared, like my performance of them, pretty weak.
Therefore I was not mortified at being chosen,
    When the teams were selected for basketball, last,
For the famous sense of fair play involved in practice
    More sense than fairness: I was neither tall nor fast.
I did not mind. I preferred standing on the sidelines
    Of athletic activities like a voyeur,
Though as I had prudently taken off my glasses
    I saw the action only as a moving blur,
Like an animated impressionistic painting,
    Till an indistinct figure detached from the rout
In pursuit of the ball bumptiously bowled me over
    With a redundant imprecation to Watch out.
I recognized him not by his voice but his odour
    Of soap now faintly diluted with healthy sweat.
While he had lurked all day on the edge of my vision,
    I had not actually spoken to him yet.
This meeting seemed an inevitable collision
    Like that of any two straight lines that intersect
Yet, when protracted to infinity grow farther
    Apart . . . I picked myself up, resigned to neglect
For the rest of the game, which seemed to last forever
    Without any further body contact at all
Between me and the other invisible players,
    Or for matter of that, between me and the ball,
Which (when I could see it) I nervously avoided

Like a taboo object with inscrutable powers.
Till the game was abruptly ended by the whistle
    Blown by our hearty coach, "That's it, men! Hit the showers!"

'Men' might sound like a flattering exaggeration
    For a bunch of barely half-grown hobbledehoys,
But this progression, from the bathtub to the showers,
    Was one of the things that distinguished men from boys,
A distinction most of them immodestly flaunted
    With a self-confidence somewhat short of supreme
As they stripped as for a primitive rite of passage
    Before disappearing into the raunchy steam.
From all this overtly goodnatured thud and blunder
    I stood apart as in a version of that dream
Wherein one appears in public uniquely naked:
    But here I was the only person partly dressed,
While perhaps the fact that I had put on my glasses
    Betrayed my shy, involuntary interest,
Which before its manifestation could be noticed
    I immediately instinctively suppressed,
Invisible as I hurriedly finished dressing
    In a free-for-all of frolicking, frisky colts
Who wielded their wet towels like offensive weapons,
    Cracking mysterious jokes about nuts and bolts.
Dressed and ready to leave, nevertheless I dawdled
    Like Lot's wife despite myself divided between
Frank curiosity and earnest disapproval
    In my attitude to the obscurely obscene.
Opposite me, Don Wisdom, adjusting his towel
    Demurely with the same disdainful nonchalance
With which he had defined a right-angle triangle,
    Did not try to hide his knowing, amused response.
At an age when good looks are so often generic
    And fugitive if not illusory, his own,
Radiant from the showers, shone with a perfection
    Peculiar to himself, as if cut in stone:
The muscular delineation of his torso
    As it were only tentatively chiselled in

Stood out in low relief against the flawless marble
    Smooth immature texture of his fair, glabrous skin.
Those features whereby I had already been smitten,
    As distinguished and as delicately defined
Now appeared as the culmination of a figure
    That Praxiteles or Myron might have designed.
Breath-taking in its splendid streamlined understatement,
    His unselfconscious, expressive near nakedness
Inspired in me such unspeakable agitation
    That I could not wait long enough to watch him dress,
But fled precipitately, my cheeks incandescent,
    My innards melting and my extremities ice,
Till I found myself on the steps of the school building,
    A fugitive from that unlikely paradise.

The grey, slate edifice, which resembled a prison
    Without as within, especially in the rain,
I soon left behind me, like the bunch at the 'bus stop,
    The girls in gay umbrellas, the boys with disdain
For the wet weather stoical in their windbreakers.
    I set out on my solitary walk home, dank
And downhill all the way. The town of New Westminster
    Where I grew up, was built on a steep river bank
And apart from an exiguous business district
    And waterfront, which were literally downtown,
Consisted mainly of modest family dwellings
    Like that in which we used to live, above the brown
And sluggish, nearly exhausted broad Fraser river
    Fraught with log-booms and fringed with filthy lumber mills,
As it crawls to the sea beyond its silt-rich delta,
    Where into the blue the polluted water spills.
(Every hero should have a river for a father;
    Appropriately, Fraser was the name of mine.
And if my character seems sadly unheroic,
    My father's nature was dubiously divine.)
On the lower slopes a few small apartment buildings
    Like the one we lived in near the library dome
Housed the unwed, widowed and orphaned, the uprooted,

Those who had lost or had never had a real home.
This domestic come-down partially motivated
    My aversion to returning to our sad flat,
Whose emptiness presented a standing temptation
    To another solitary practice than that
Of our upright and badly out of tune piano.
    To my hard-won chastity it seemed as if sex,
Misconceived and repudiated, lay in ambush
    Everywhere: even the landscape was rated X;
Nor could I be comforted by the observation
    That my by and large irrational sense of sin
Derived, not from blameless and indifferent nature,
    But from my imagination its origin.

Not altogether. My revery was truncated
    By rude reality in the unpleasing shape
Of a gradeschool playmate who hailed me gaily with a
    Familiarity which I would fain escape:
A former neighbour and occasional accomplice,
    For I had not always been such a goody-good,
Indeed I had been deemed the ingenious ringleader
    Of forbidden games in my childhood neighbourhood.
Not having seen much of him since, I was astonished
    By how overgrown and oafish he had become.
That he did not notice my moral reformation
    I thought natural in one so depraved and dumb,
As he asked me to a clandestine get-together
    Of the gang: "It's more fun when everyone can come."
To document his case he pulled from his pocket
    A dirty, well-thumbed, and well-fingered funny book,
The Boy's Own Manual, at which, when it was brandished
    In my face, I ostensibly refused to look,
Shuddering, but in my righteous repudiation
    Failed to sense the insidious seed of regret
That once sown would grow to bear bitter fruit thereafter.
    In years to come I might be sorry, but not yet.
Meanwhile, puzzled by my unsolicited lecture
    On the evils of sex, my tempter said, "Forget

It! I'll just tell the other guys that you can't make it."
    But my pompous last words were, "Say I've put such kid
Stuff behind me." He shrugged, "You don't know what you're missing..."
    As he trotted off. The trouble was that I did.

For the moment I had succeeded in postponing
    What I feared must be my inevitable fall,
Cause enough for premature self-congratulation,
    Yet might not love prevail where lust was bound to fail?
Singlehanded I had to deduce the distinction
    From limited experience. Lust, if diffuse,
Dedicated itself to a practical object;
    Singleminded love appeared of no earthly use.
Exhilarated by the temporary triumph
    Of chastity, but still leery of solitude
Lest, withstanding the blandishments of bad companions,
    I succumb to my own complacent rectitude,
I directed my steps in search of sanctuary
    From myself, toward my favourite habitat
Among the open shelves of the public library
    A short block away from our unwelcoming flat.
There, having graduated from the children's section
    Already, I greedily foraged through adult
Books that, while hardly in a more modern sense Adult,
    Sometimes produced the same deplorable result.
Perceiving no way of escaping altogether
    The way of all flesh, no matter how hard I tried,
I was brought up short by the sudden apparition
    In front of me of Don Wisdom erect astride
His bicycle, its basket stuffed with rolled-up papers
    To be delivered. He muttered, "You want a ride?"
With a careless air implying Take it or leave it,
    Impatiently, barely glancing at me askance.
Yet these, his second words to me—the first were, "Watch it!"
    Sounded almost an invitation to the dance.
Except in the most exceptional circumstances
    From one boy to another this might be thought queer.
Why not? A proposal is not a proposition,

And from Wisdom I sensed I had nothing to fear;
So I clambered aboard his unbalanced contraption
    And joined him in his erratic downhill career.

Squeezed in front of him uncomfortably astraddle
    Between his pedalling legs and the handlebars,
I saw flash past the blocks that I had trudged that morning
    As he cut corners and careened about parked cars.
He had to reach around me to get each newspaper
    He threw, without stopping, onto somebody's lawn.
When I admired his aim, which was not quite unerring,
    He laughed: "You ought to see me do it before dawn."
I wondered then how many disgruntled subscribers
    Have any idea how fortunate they are,
As they retrieve their daily papers from the bushes,
    To have The Evening Sun brought by the morning star?
For so he appeared to me, my imagination
    Already by my reading of Blake so enflamed
That I did not care if the splendid Son of Morning
    Alias Lucifer was sinisterly named.
By his presence, indeed proximity, imprisoned,
    As well as by the headlong rate at which we went,
I fell silent as long as we continued moving,
    Abashed by the facility of our descent,
Discomfited by our unavoidable contact,
    Gripped in the vice of his mechanical embrace,
Desperately I tried to concentrate on nothing
    But the fine rain that carelessly caressed my face.
Throughout that thrilling, all too terminable joy-ride,
    Transparent as an icecube, I thought I should melt
Under the influence of intemperate feelings,
    But I could not have told anyone how I felt.
I suppose I might attempt a better description
    Now than then, for like most sensation-seeking teens,
Or for that matter the majority of mankind,
    I thought experience an end and not a means,
A dead end as a rule, and had not yet discovered
    The means whereby imagination can transcend

Momentary often disappointing impressions,
    Or that art that becomes itself a living end.

Be that as it may, equally speechless and breathless,
    He braked to a stop as unforeseen as our start
On a windy corner where his dismissive gesture
    Indicated we must temporarily part.
So far not having inquired where I was going,
    He pointed out his route down the glistening street
And asked where I lived. When I said, in an apartment,
    He exclaimed with wide-eyed envy, "That must be neat!"
I had to admit that the flat was fairly tidy—
    I might have preferred a cosy domestic mess—
But he added, "It must be like being a grown-up,
    On your lonesome." And I miserably nodded, Yes.
Cleanliness no less than loneliness seemed a symptom
    Of my sick mother's absence: an excellent cook,
But indifferent housekeeper, she spent her lifetime
    On the sofa with a cigarette and a book,
Which she used to put down indulgently the moment
    I returned from school, to give full attention to
My narratives, which she preferred to a novel
    In part because she knew they were perfectly true.
Hence my aforesaid, unmentionable reluctance
    To return to our empty flat, the scene of both
An enviable yet unwelcome independence
    And the more unacceptable aspects of growth.
Strangely, Don Wisdom's mute presence alleviated
    The pangs of not only solitude but desire,
As if the proximity of real flesh extinguished
    Fantasy's self-satisfied and fatuous fire.
I did not for a moment fancy he was feeling
    Anything like what I did, certainly not yet,
Still we prolonged our inarticulate leave-taking,
    All the more awkward because we had barely met.
"Well, so long, See you around. I'd better be going."
    "Thanks for the lift." But despite our manly display
Of indifferent restraint, we bashfully dallied,
    Unable or unwilling to call it a day,

While the waning Autumn afternoon also lingered,
    Malingered rather, feigning an early decline
Behind the hidden mountains that ringed the horizon
    Which emerged from hiding when the weather turned fine.
Then without further ado or adieux, unsmiling
    He mounted his bike and pedalled off down the block,
While I watched him out of sight, long after he vanished
    As gratuitously as he had appeared, stock
Still, as if rooted to the spot. Just so does Ovid
    Describe Daphne or Hyacinth transformed by the god
Without warning into their vegetative namesakes;
    And I wonder if they too found anything odd
In their sudden immobility, the sensation
    Of aching into leaf? No more could I explain
Or halt my instantaneous metamorphosis
    With its dumb bewilderment and burgeoning pain.

OCTOBER: HALLOWE'EN

Where to begin now that the narrative beginning
    Lies behind us? The middle of the mixed-up years
When every new act seems like an initiation
    Which one impatiently anticipates and fears.
The first cigarette or kiss, words in a weird language
    Whose strange vocabulary suits a changing voice,
Presuppose something quite unthinkable in childhood,
    The capacity, and necessity, for choice.
Then was it so, and did it actually happen
    As the fond narrator imagines? Not a bit,
Since all narrative shares the tendency of fiction,
    Long-winded and naturalistic, to omit
So much of what weaves the warped texture of existence
    Plus any unaesthetic facts that do not fit,
Like the pervasive, unsubtle hothouse aroma
    Of longing that made puberty such a living hell,
Which the most candid camera cannot recapture—
    Snapshots in a family album do not smell—
And which the pen is criticised for reproducing
    With a fidelity gross enough to repel
The reader who has not altogether forgotten
    How hard it was when the prurient frontispiece
Of the book of life, peeked at, seemed hectically coloured
    By desires denied all immediate release.
The truest account resembles a mistranslation;
    Description tends automatically to betray,
Living and telling such separate enterprises,
    Who can perform his life as if it were a play?
Not I, for one, but the unaccountable feeling
    Afflicted me at moments of crisis that, gripped
As I was by sincere emotions, I was acting,
    Though I sometimes wondered who had written the script.
An invented, arbitrary approximation
    The name of a thing and that thing are not the same;

Life, a functional illiterate, with a flourish
    Always makes its mark but cannot sign its full name.

In the weeks that followed our initial encounter,
    If I saw less of Don Wisdom than I might wish,
I was not his only worshipper from a distance,
    Since he was what the girls in Home Ec. called "a dish"—
Not that I should myself have personally chosen
    Such a homely, anthropophagic metaphor
For what seemed to me a supernatural vessel,
    The Holy Grail whom I had been questing for,
Unconsciously of course. He resembled the hero
    In an interminable childish fantasy
Wherein a dashing and goodlooking young daredevil
    Befriended and instructed and protected me
Through a bedtime series of hair-raising adventures
    In the course of which he sometimes got slightly hurt,
Which necessitated not only tender nursing
    But the removal of my brave rescuer's shirt.
Strange to relate, it was not early adolescence
    But latency elaborated this romance:
Teaching myself to read when I was very little,
    The first name I figured out was Prince Valiant's.

In fact the daily distance between me and Wisdom
    While not quite as astronomical as appears
In retrospect, grew in proportion as our orbits
    Diverged; we revolved in incompatible spheres,
His enlarged, and indeed pneumatically inflated
    Like its social focus the ubiquitous ball,
Mine, although it certainly did not lack a centre,
    Having practically no circumference at all.
Ashamed to acknowledge our acquaintance in public,
    He still granted me the odd, astonishing gift
Of a word or a look when he thought no one was looking,
    But never again did he offer me a lift.

Normally talkative, suddenly in his presence
    I found myself tongue-tied and abnormally shy,

Yet I sought out each occasion of wordless torment,
    Too devoted and still too dumb to wonder why
Any such thing as unreciprocated friendship
    Was a contradiction; normal affection must
Be mutual, and liking, which is based on likeness,
    Lacks the disinterestedness of love, or lust.
My feelings, too vague and delicate for the latter,
    Apparently pure, however suspect their source,
Were shocked that so much lofty romantic emotion
    Should come down in the end to carnal intercourse.
My indefinite day-dreams were illuminated
    By a dream one night that explained as plain as day
The basic nature of my desires in explicit
    Imagery which I could not explicate away
On awaking. Surprisingly sophisticated—
    More than I knew—yet excruciatingly crude,
I could not record, if I remembered, the details,
    Except that Don and I were together and nude.
In vain I strove to deny my natural instincts
    In face of the naked nocturnal evidence.
So this was it! the sensational guilty secret
    Sentimentalized by my half-baked innocence!
Startled to realize that my love had any object
    Beyond contemplation, which I never tired of,
But short of the casual give-and-take of friendship,
    The marvel is that I came to label it love.
I could say nothing to my unwitting beloved
    Of course: no way that I was about to confide
Enormities that he might have understood better
    Than the devotion I made no attempt to hide.
At the same time I could not refrain from regarding
    His blameless face in a less innocuous light,
The pure features that I adored in class each morning
    Attached to the body I had possessed last night.
Ironically, given my lack of self-possession,
    I was by love or its understudy possessed,
Our dream intimacy mocked by the waking vision
    In which I saw my sleeping partner fully dressed.
Moreover a sort of emotional hangover,

A guilty depression like a psychic headache
Blighted relations with my oneiric accomplice
    During our infrequent chance meetings when awake.
For some reason, even as our nocturnal contacts
    Grew ever more and more unambiguous,
Our daily dealings remained externally frigid
    So no knowing observer could have fingered us
As love-birds, for which a coarser term was more common—
    Nor were we, of course, except in the cage of dreams,
But I sometimes wondered if his imagination
    Entertained variations on similar themes.
I doubted it. As it was, my baffled attraction
    Found surreptitious outlet in a sheepish look,
Most often ignored, that must when intercepted,
    Have been as open as the library book
That always lay on my lap in class, and which teachers
    Usually were blind enough to overlook.
As a token of maturity or machismo
    At an age when sports become more manly than games,
It was unthinkable for self-respecting schoolboys
    To address one another by their given names,
The use of the more formal, impersonal surname
    Being repeated as a shibboleth or sign
Of status; so on the significant occasions
    When he spoke to me, Don Wisdom did so by mine:
As if shy of the endearment latent in Daryl,
    He kept me at arm's length with the brush-off of Hine.
But while I referred to him in public as Wisdom
    In my secret reveries he figured as Don;
Between the nominative and vocative cases
    Lay a radical distinction; besides he shone
In my wretched, ignorant, emotional darkness
    With the pristine, radiant beauty of the dawn—
Of wisdom? or what I should learn the world called folly?
    I did not quibble during the dismal dark night
Of my senses at the source of illumination,
    Intoxicated at the ambiguous light.
I found in its contemplation a heady sweetness,
    Touching in the soul a new erogenous zone,

And at a time of estrangement and transformation
    Something precious to appropriate as my own.
This feeling, all the more priceless for being secret,
    Provided me with something positive to cling
To: it was like opening a window in Winter
    And exclaiming, with Sieglinde, "You are the Spring."

Unacquainted with the clinical nomenclature,
    Which would seem to me irrelevant anyway,
I could not accept the glib vernacular verdict
    That might have labelled me as queer, (no one said 'gay'
In those days): a charge I must have repudiated
    Insofar as my crush was evidently chaste.
In the vulgar view unnatural affections,
    Like natural functions, belonged below the waist.
And yet queerness was not primarily a question,
    In common parlance, of those questionable acts
Which were bandied about by show-offs in the showers
    Fumbling with the slippery, fascinating facts
Of life; rather it was a matter of the manner
    In which a boy carried his books or cut his hair.
A queer was no more nor less than a noncomformist,
    A heretic at whom girls would giggle and stare
Because he had a coiffure longer than a crew-cut
    Or held his books in front instead of at his side,
Or broke the unwritten code of custom and costume
    By any refinement condemned as sissified.
One paradoxical hallmark of the true sissy
    Was excessive contact with the opposite sex,
While voluntary segregation of the genders
    Constituted a stand-off that used to perplex
Me in view of their mutual preoccupation,
    If all the heterosexual poppycock
I had to overhear were any indication,
    Not just, as I suspected, a lot of loose talk.
Strangely enough, although an obvious outsider,
    I was never, for reasons not hard to explain,
Ostracized as a social or sexual misfit,
    Largely because I was held in awe as a 'brain',

And was it not common knowledge that brains are sexless,
    As well as inept at such things as shop and gym,
Dismissed, with a mixture of respect and derision,
    As odd, awkward, and asexual seraphim?

Oddly grateful for the myth that emasculated
    Me, I soon introjected that myth as a lie,
(As mythical truth dictates historical falsehood),
    And invoked public opinion to stifle my
Inadmissible if not universal yearnings,
    Without hypocrisy, for there was no pretense:
I really tried to deny what Blake celebrated,
    The sexuality of the intelligence.
Nor was it a mere societal solecism
    I sought to avoid so much as sex as such;
My desires, while aborted, seemed to me quite normal,
    But I put out of mind what tact put out of touch.
Unfamiliar with the concept of sublimation,
    Yet hopelessly hooked on what I saw as sublime,
It did not occur to me that something so high-minded
    In the eyes of society could be a crime.
There was nothing remotely queer about Don Wisdom,
    To all outward appearances perfectly straight
As the shortest distance between two points, a short-cut
    From which he did not seem likely to deviate.
Oblivious to his rectilinear beauty
    Apparently, stand-offish without seeming shy,
He managed despite his exceptional distinction
    With no effort to pass for a regular guy.

If it be objected that I have fixed my focus
    Too exclusively on the school environment,
School looks like life to a sheltered middle-class youngster,
    While life is school to a rowdier element,
All the more so as, not being boarding-school inmates,
    We were let out at end of the short school day.
I often wondered why in the circumstances
    My sorely-tried father did not send me away
To one of the few private but hardly exclusive

Pseudo-British barracks with their quaint uniforms
And emphasis on cricket, classics and cold showers,
　　Manliness, religion, and ragging in the dorms—
At least according to all the fictional sources
　　I had consulted; but I could merely surmise
His motives included paternal parsimony
　　And pride, for he could not afford to patronize
Professionally, as a pillar or pilaster
　　Of public education, the alternative.
Privately I was not sorry. When school was over
　　The public library was where I used to live
The extracurricular and inner existence
　　That was my principal excuse for a real life.
Our present home seemed less invitingly domestic
　　Without the presence of a mother and a wife.
Compared to the cosy circumstances of childhood,
　　Which although comfortable had been far from grand,
Day by day the modest efficiency apartment
　　Seemed like my life to contract rather than expand,
My claustrophobia augmented by awaiting
　　Inevitable word confirming the demise
Of her whose picture from the top of the piano
　　Followed me with infinitely reproachful eyes.
These sadly overcrowded new living conditions
　　Served to underline our lapse from domestic grace,
Like old folks' rooms, where the furniture of a lifetime
　　Is crammed into an exiguous rented space,
Higgledy-piggledy, memories too expensive
　　To get rid of, yet inconvenient to keep,
Gathering dust, useless, unwanted and unnoticed,
　　Their sole property the power to make one weep.
The living room, listlessly haunted by the living,
　　The spotless kitchenette in which my father prepared
And we consumed our tasteless fare and washed the dishes,
　　The pokey bedroom that we uneasily shared:
Home was the place in which I rarely did my homework
　　And far from the setting for a real heart-to-heart,
Suggesting that in probability apartment
　　Must derive etymologically from *apart*.

The more unavoidable our physical nearness,
 The further apart father and I seemed to dwell,
Till we became like two incompatible convicts
 Compelled to share the same inhospitable cell,
Divided rather than united by our common
 Sorrow, of which it was unthinkable to speak.
My father reproved all emotional expression
 As indecent and—more reprehensible—weak.
But while he played the stiff-upper-lipped Scottish stoic
 Cast in the fine old inflexible Roman mould,
The consolations of philosophy could offer
 Cold comfort to a grief-stricken thirteen-year-old.
Yet I must give him credit with being consistent:
 Even in old age he repeats the same refrain
In reply to my variations on 'How are you?'
 Discouraging further sympathy, "Can't complain."
As much as his studied mastery of meiosis,
 This courageous but somewhat frigid attitude,
While setting me an inimitable example
 Only succeeded in sealing my solitude.
So, returning from his short, semi-weekly visits
 To my mother, whom I was not allowed to see
Any more, he would merely shake his head and mutter,
 "It won't be long now. She is sinking visibly."
He made me feel there was something about her dying
 Unspeakably disreputable, like divorce,
So in addition to inexpressible sorrow
 I was burdened by inexplicable remorse.
Since it was all my fault, I thought, for being naughty,
 I resolved to be good henceforth—perhaps too late—
What's more succeeding in this silent resolution
 To the extent that I soon ceased to masturbate,
No mean feat at that age, without parental guidance,
 For my father, plainly finding the facts of life
Unpalatable, had left their elucidation
 For as long as possible to his dying wife.
Strange that for one so avowedly realistic
 Certain unmentionable things did not exist!
But he ignored both the painful and the unpleasant

As complacently as a Christian Scientist.
With the suppression of sex and death and self-pity
    We had nothing of much interest to discuss.
Emotionally in the absence of my mother
    The nuclear family lost its nucleus,
Leaving us like unaffiliated electrons
    In meaningless orbit about a central void,
Approaching only at the risk of a collision,
    Which we were equally determined to avoid.

My father, a magisterial man of fifty,
    Only a few years older than I am today,
Looked, I was told, much the same as he had at thirty,
    The age at which his hair turned prematurely grey—
Nor has he changed beyond recognition at eighty:
    These valetudinarians know how to live!
In appearance, as in political conviction,
    A staunchly unimpeachable conservative,
A moss-backed, reactionary, true blue-nosed Tory,
    Yet no adherent of the radical right,
Quixotically defending traditional values
    In a civilization sprung up overnight,
British Columbia, discovered by his kinsman
    Simon Fraser barely a century ago.
Conservatives qualified themselves as Progressive
    In a climate where customs melt as fast as snow.
In local circles my father passed for old-fashioned
    If not positively antediluvian,
His palaeolithic prejudices respected
    As crochets quintessentially Canadian.
More a pedagogic than a domestic despot,
    Wielding an authority absolute but mild,
He ruled by psychological intimidation;
    It was left to my mother to chastise the child.
One of Fraser's favourite forms of subtle torture
    Used devices designed to measure my I.Q.,
Tests he used to bring home from school; competitively,
    While he administered them he would take them too.

Night after night, seated across the kitchen table,
    Paternal pride contended with personal pique
When I threw down my pencil. "What? Finished already?"
    He would not tell me my score, but I sneaked a peek.
As elementary school principal and teacher,
    One who exacted unthinking obedience,
My father sought to check the vagaries of talent
    In the name of something he called common sense,
A conventional, unimaginative virtue
    That the bourgeoisie historically idolized,
The stolid antitheses of those superstitions
    Which the unruly gifted young have always prized.
To this drab but insatiably blood-thirsty Moloch
    How many promising lives have been sacrificed?
If I escaped, and then only for the time being,
    It was to be at an incalculable price.

One dismal October afternoon two years later
    I had hurried straight home from school all eagerness
To tinker with the verse whose sloppy composition
    Created what my father deplored as a mess
On my makeshift desk; I found the space devastated
    Like a battlefield which the despoiler has stripped,
And looking out the window I beheld my father
    Feeding the flames of a bonfire with manuscript.
When confronted by me across this conflagration
    He said he had found some meaninglessly inked
Scraps of waste paper cluttering up the cardtable.
    I sneered, "I thought Neanderthal man was extinct."
What I said at the time and what I did thereafter,
    However decisive, are neither here nor there;
What does seem strange is that when I left home forever
    I should leave my juvenilia in his care,
To be faintly surprised when, questioned long thereafter,
    He said that it had vanished into empty air.
Once when I was younger, recovering from measles,
    Forbidden to read and bored with childish board games,
Mother gave me a book of paper dolls to cut out

Which father also consecrated to the flames.
Justifying his penchant for incineration,
    He swore no son of his would be a pantywaist,
Thus scotching my future as a fashion designer
    As he later sought to scorch my poetic taste.

On the whole I suppose that I ought to feel grateful
    For such drastic discouragement, doubtless well meant.
How much promise have I not seen annihilated
    By excessive fond parental encouragement!
There is nothing like despicable opposition
    To stiffen the determination of a lad,
So I owe my lifelong literary persistence
    To the rational disapproval of my dad.
He resembled in his paternal perturbation
    A duck or hen or some other domestic fowl
Who finds after weeks of dutiful incubation
    That it has hatched out a nightingale or an owl.
Of either you might say all I lacked were the feathers,
    Though I was a fledgling of a different kind,
My owlish appearance due to the horn-rimmed glasses
    I wore, without which I was practically blind.
In those days spectacles had none of the cosmetic
    Glamour of today when frames are fashion-designed;
Myopia was a stigma; but interested
    More in seeing than being seen, I used to mind
The epithet "four-eyes" less than the reputation,
    Totally unearned in fact, of being a "grind".
Not that I should have denied I was a bookworm,
    But to the bibliophobe all books look alike;
Thus Fraser was dismayed when for my thirteenth birthday
    I had opted for a book instead of a bike,
Unreasonably disappointed that at that awkward
    Age any healthy boy would rather read than to ride.
With the distrust of letters of an educator
    He was always telling me to go play outside,
Often characteristically misquoting Wordsworth
    Until I wondered if what that pantheist meant

By books in trees was that each week a virgin forest
    Was felled for an educational supplement?

Making a virtue of necessity, my practice
    In the absence of bike or 'bus fare was to walk
To and from school; at noon I avoided the lunch room
    In favour of the open air, shunning foul talk.
In those days there were plenty of secluded places
    For a sensitive boy to get off on his own,
And I haunted the beauty spots in which our city
    Abounded, never less alone than when alone,
In the course of my erratic perambulations
    Stumbling across many an unfrequented nook,
Where undeterred by the damp climatic conditions
    I could immerse myself breathlessly in a book.
Still the world, that vast interlineated volume
    Full of unsettling, illegible evidence,
As fascinating and upsetting as graffiti,
    Was insensibly just beginning to make sense.
This manuscript was gaudily illuminated
    With scarlet and yellow and bronze and tarnished gold,
Though not so colourful, I found, as Eastern woodlands,
    Perhaps because our winters were not half so cold,
But partly as the conifers that dominated
    The magnificent but rather oppressive scene,
Instead of frivolously changing with the season
    Remain a sober, disheartening dark green.
The most British thing about British Columbia,
    Namely the weather, which was temperate but dank,
May explain the strain of romantic melancholy
    For which it has the Japanese current to thank.

The death of the year merely mirrored my depression.
    Prematurely, perhaps, I had begun to grieve
For my missing and moribund mother in secret.
    So that year going abroad on All Hallows' Eve
Seemed out of the question: mocked by jolly hobgoblins
    And by jack-o-lanterns with their meaningless grin,

OCTOBER

Writhing alive in the purgatorial bonfire
  Of puberty, I was not about to begin
(Even had I been invited) bobbing for apples
  Or dressing up, as hitherto, in a white sheet,
Shopping bag in hand to beg the neighbours for candy,
  Too old to be interested in trick or treat.
Was I becoming myself a mythical monster,
  The kind of which I had been taught to be afraid?
How gruesome to outgrow one's innocent illusions
  And glimpse the ghastly truth behind the masquerade:
That we are the playthings of the powers of darkness.
  The dead cannot be raised, but few ghosts may be laid.

NOVEMBER: ALL SOULS' DAY

Is it wrong to imagine a dreaded disaster,
　　When at last it befalls, will come as a relief?
For in fact the agony of anticipation
　　Cannot compare to the extremity of grief.
Too exclusive a concentration on the future
　　Which after all remains strictly a non-event,
While alleviating the rigours of the present,
　　Can only end in chronic disillusionment.
The impatient expectation of adolescents
　　And their obsession with the shape of things to come,
Like the animal knack for living in the moment,
　　Strike the experienced as ultimately dumb.
At the same time, while it is probably unhealthy,
　　As my father insisted, to dwell in the past,
Is that not better than the pragmatic amnesia
　　Of the instant sentimental iconoclast?
Time is like an uninhabited haunted castle
　　All of whose doors may be unlocked except the last.

Early on the morning of the sixth of November
　　The hospital called to say that my mother had died,
And although the end had been far from unexpected
　　At the tidings of her death I childishly cried.
My father, who received the telephonic message
　　In silence, at a loss for something kind to say,
Resorted to an all too common euphemism
　　In breaking the news to me: "She passed away."
And there seemed something surreptitious in her passing,
　　As if she had decamped or simply disappeared,
Word of which arrived as a cruel anticlimax,
　　The confirmation of what had been so long feared.
The ultimate departure daily apprehended,
　　The blow anticipated with no hope for weeks
When it fell left me feeling physically assaulted,

The evidence of grief unblotted on my cheeks.
The bulletin came when, having just finished breakfast,
    We were washing dishes and putting them away.
I remember that, as usual, it was raining;
    Since there was no school, it must have been Saturday.
Informed, I immediately fled to the bedroom
    And knelt with my wet face against the tartan spread
Till presently recalled to the land of the living,
    Like it or not, by my father's firm Spartan tread.
His off-hand manner of administering comfort,
    Which he must have needed himself, distant and gruff,
Rebuked my tearful exhibition as excessive
    If not wholly inexcusable: "That's enough."
A little tenderness, not to mention indulgence,
    Might have seemed in order for one bereaved so young,
But my father dismissed my manifest affliction
    As an hysterical symptom: I was "high-strung",
Which may be a virtue in a violincello
    Or other sensitive instruments that are kept
At a certain pitch, but not in an adolescent.
    Henceforward I must weep by myself when I wept.
Was there something sick in this solitary mourning,
    Morbidly selfconscious though certainly sincere,
As if with a desperate but specious detachment
    I questioned the credentials of my every tear,
Thus casting the sickening shadow of suspicion
    Across the stricken inner landscape of my grief,
Adding to genuine unhappiness the extra,
    Quite unnecessary burden of disbelief?
Trapped in a state of almost hallucinatory
    Shock-induced clarity, I prayed for a mistake,
Knowing there was none, no way out of the true nightmare
    All the more horrible since I was wide awake.

When I say I prayed, I tried what all human beings
    In all ages and places have done in despair,
Alternative to an eternity of weeping
    Testing the advertised efficacy of prayer.
In the course of a spotty religious education

The childish practice of saying God Bless each night
Had been neglected in favour of much high-minded
    Protestant nonsense about moral wrong and right.
My father, a sceptical, erratic church-goer
    Regarded religion as a secular rite;
My mother, who had more heart-felt religious leanings
    Of the vague but cosy old low Anglican kind,
Dying in a Roman Catholic institution
    Was surprised, she told me on one visit, to find
The black-clad votaresses of the Scarlet Woman
    She was brought up to detest, so cheerful and kind.
My visits to the hospital were dominated
    By an incongruously life-like crucifix;
On the way out I used to help myself to pamphlets
    Explaining the beliefs of Roman Catholics.
With titles like, *Prayer, Penitence and Purgatory,*
    The Doctrine of the Real Presence, The One True Church,
Militant or Triumphant? which I read covertly
    Like dirty books in bed, till this furtive research
Was terminated by my disapproving father
    When he burnt that propaganda as he would burn
My verse and had burnt those inoffensive cut-outs:
    From the Inquisition he had little to learn!
Nevertheless, or perhaps therefore, I continued
    Curious concerning the preposterous claims
That under the Counter-reformation's exotic
    Baroque facade would have sentenced me to the flames.
As far as I know my mother never converted
    To the promulgations of the Council of Trent,
Even on her death bed reportedly rereading,
    Like a good Protestant, the English Testament,
Which after her death was found at the bedside open
    To the beginning of the fourth gospel, I heard,
As if she hoped that in her end was her beginning
    And that, if so, in the beginning was the word.

While it did not mark the commencement of our mourning
    Which dated from the diagnosis of No Hope,
Death inaugurated innumerable duties

With which father had not ungratefully to cope,
Offering as they did legitimate distraction
    If not consolation to the busy bereaved;
But I with no such lugubrious occupation
    To dull or dignify bereavement, simply grieved,
Afflicted by visits and letters of condolence
    As difficult to receive as to write and pay.
It is notoriously painful in the presence
    Of desolation to find anything to say,
Yet such rituals have the necessary function
    Of distancing us somewhat from the dear deceased,
From the tastefulness of the funeral arrangements
    To the tastelessness of the funereal feast.
The headstone, of pink British Columbian granite,
    Was inscribed with mother's name and chronology,
1900–1949, and the faintly
    Hypocritical epitaph, *Abide with me.*
Of these onerous, unavoidable expenses
    Fraser, who bore them, had every right to complain:
First the hospital, then the funeral and graveyard
    Created (he grumbled) a grave financial drain;
It looked as if he would be paying for poor mother
    For ever, or at least till he married again.
That he would do so I already took for granted,
    Of course after a respectable interval;
And he would be just as faithful to her successor:
    For father's infidelities were serial.
Uxorious to a fault, he could not imagine
    Let alone long support a single, widowed life,
Which was all very well for him. Unfortunately
    A mother is less replaceable than a wife.

Following that first, incommunicado weekend,
    I was kept home, sequestered, all week long from school,
As if in quarantine. Lest grief should be contagious
    All but family visits were against the rule.
I was ashamed to wonder, if I had been summoned
    Suddenly during class, would Don have been impressed
By someone to whom something untoward had happened,

An object less of pity than of interest?
As it was, in the mute company of the upright
    Shut-up piano I too was shut up and mute,
Absorbed in a protracted, monotonous mourning
    For her whose chronic absence had become acute.
Until the funeral her death was an abstraction
    Whose magnitude I finally began to grasp
When, paraded hastily past the open casket,
    I recognized her ghastly likeness with a gasp
And a glance at the lifelike mask of that cadaver,
    A waxy sample of the undertaker's tact,
She who never wore make-up so vividly painted
    I had to accept her extinction as a fact.
Thus it was not until I saw her in her coffin
    That I could believe my mother was really dead,
And even so I knew that she would live forever,
    If not in heaven as the minister glibly said,
A sadly diminished, dim, posthumous existence
    In the Pandora's box of memory instead.
Fashions in funerals have changed like any other.
    At the last I attended the coffin was closed;
But the barbaric practice of viewing the body
    Proved more cathartic than I at the time supposed.
How could one, without the final confrontation,
    Acknowledge our loss and properly say goodbye,
This effigy from which the person had absconded
    Allowing me without selfconsciousness to cry
Till I could no longer see those floral arrangements
    Bizarrely inappropriate to funerals,
Like life in the midst of death—for what are cut flowers
    In fact but colourful, castrated genitals?
Such unwelcome biological observations
    Only added to my ineffable distress,
As did the presence of my heartless Aunt Lachesis
    At the graveside in a frivolous floral dress,
One of the trio of my mother's younger sisters
    Whom she had helped bring up after their father died
In a mine disaster, leaving their mother helpless.
    At the age of eighteen my mother had qualified

As a teacher just in time to support a widow
    And three orphans, God knows how on her modest pay.
Gathered today for her obsequies, they reminded
    Me of the fates, literally what people say.

The closest in age and appearance to my mother
    I shall call Clotho, though she neither toiled nor span
At her silvan hideaway on Vancouver Island,
    Married to a French-Canadian lumberman.
In the absence of electricity and plumbing
    She liked to posture as a backwoods chatelaine.
Uncle Yves did the cooking and her half-grown daughters
    Did the housework, leaving her free to entertain
The few neighbours at musical evening parties
    Where she both played and sang, my mother said, off-key.
With her embonpoint she lacked her sister's good nature
    And satiric sense of her own absurdity.
Aunt Atropos, in contrast, dwelt in a suburban
    Bungalow not even family was allowed
To enter without removing footwear beforehand
    As if in a mosque, she was so very house-proud.
Although her husband worked as a streetcar conductor,
    She preferred to refer airily to his job
As "something high-up in urban mass transportation",
    And was derided by my mother for a snob.
Now as mother's nearest living female relation—
    Living nearest in a geographical sense—
It was her chore to sort through her dead sister's wardrobe
    For my father, removing the stale evidence
Of a lifetime in the shape of the shapeless dresses
    Hung in the closet like Bluebeard's forsaken wives,
Suggesting that, when personality has perished,
    Usually the discarded garment survives.
When I clung fetishistically to a kimono
    My disapproving aunt briskly took it away;
I was too old for dressing up, she said, moreover
    She could not imagine what my father would say.
Reluctantly I relinquished the sacred memento.
    The reiterated injunction to be brave

Meant shunning anything morbid or sentimental,
    So I was forbidden to visit mother's grave.

Her youngest and once favourite sister, Lachesis
    Was a red-head of whom we did not see a lot
Since she had married an Irish Catholic, the catspaw,
    My grandmother darkly claimed, of a Popish plot.
My mother's mother, whom I may as well call Themis
    (Though she was prejudiced as most provincials are)
Supplemented her inadequate widow's pension
    By going out to work, cheerfully, as a char.
Such my maternal relatives, here represented
    In the threadbare allegory of ancient myth;
But no less mythical is the name of her birthplace
    Around the turn of the century: Ladysmith.
Despite which impressive Victorian beginnings
    She did not become a United Empire Loyalist,
But the citizen of a democratic country
    Where no class distinctions in principle exist,
An egalitarianism contradicted
    In practice invidiously in the first grade
Where discrimination between bluebirds and robins
    Constituted a pecking-order ready-made,
Not as primitive perhaps as that of the playground,
    But more important, if doubtless no less unfair,
Dictating as it did the high school one would go to,
    And later the colour of collar one would wear.
As a teacher the division mother acknowledged
    Was not between those who had and those who had not
Whatever it might be, but between the consumers
    Who docilely learned, and the producers who taught.
My upbringing in such an upright pedagogic
    Environment surely suffices to explain,
Apart from my putative genetic endowment,
    My own deep, irrepressible didactic strain.
So mother in a series of one-room schoolhouses
    Here and there in the hinterlands that are B.C.'s
Heartland, so immense and beautiful and yet empty,
    Taught immigrants and indigenes their A.B.C.'s.

By the time all her dependent siblings were settled
    In life, which is to say married, she found herself
Nearing thirty without matrimonial prospects,
    Which at that epoch meant pretty much on the shelf.
At this critical juncture along came my father.
    An unwounded survivor of the First World War,
Her age, he too was an elementary school teacher
    And, more important, an unconfirmed bachelor.
While their courtship took place during the "roaring twenties",
    In Canada even the 'twenties did not roar.
The path of true love ran irregular as always—
    We dig our own pitfalls when adversity fails—
For some reason in the middle of the engagement
    Fraser embarked on a freighter for New South Wales.
Halfway across the Pacific the vessel foundered
    And drifted for weeks before rescue, her son's plight
Described in daily bulletins in lieu of wireless
    By my Highland grandmother who claimed second sight.
Returned, Fraser behaved as if nothing had happened—
    A disarming, and unnerving, habit he had—
And embraced his preordained career as a husband
    In the course of which he was to become my dad,
But not according to the normal course of nature,
    As I discovered when I was finally told
What I had already guessed, that I was adopted.
    Confirmation when I was about ten years old
Of one of the commonest fantasies of childhood
    Which in my case proved all too traumatically true,
This left me with the uncomfortable suspicion
    That my other, secret fears would be confirmed too.
Though my mother explained that as I had been chosen
    I was wanted more than some children she could name
And I believed her, I did not find this much comfort
    At the time: elective love was not quite the same.
But what was I to call her anyway but mother?
    She embodied to perfection that common noun,
Who when I was a malnourished, abandoned infant
    Picked me up and swore she would never put me down.
Too young at the time of her death to use her proper

Name, which was Elsie, as another grown-up would,
How can I portray her save in the hieratic
Sentimentally frozen pose of motherhood?
If it puzzles me to picture her as a person
Apart from my own self-centred infantile wants,
What child has any real conception of his parents
Except in terms of their responsible response?
Deprived by death of that independent perspective
Which might have come with age, though then not easily,
My view of my mother was forever arrested,
Like my father's anachronistic view of me.
What I remember is a large, comforting presence
And an effortless, unfailing intimacy.

An impressive, generously proportioned woman,
Imposing in the shabbiest cotton housedress,
She was a far cry from a fanatical housewife,
Her environment an often edible mess.
I see her where she was most at home, in the kitchen,
Concocting some sinfully high-calorie treat,
Cakes or pies or cookies, fudge or muffins or creampuffs
To tempt a tooth that even then was none too sweet;
Or extended, immense, on the chesterfield, reading—
What she used to describe as "putting up her feet"—
With a pot of tea and an ashtray at her elbow:
Sometimes I believe she would rather read than eat.
No wonder, then, that I grew up not only chubby
But literate, literally omnivorous,
The butt of much ill-natured teasing by my skinny
Schoolmates, who mother said were merely envious.
Like the heroine's in a novel by Jane Austen
Her marital life might have proved a happy blank,
Had it not been for my fortuitous existence,
For which I have her former childlessness to thank.
She had on her marriage of course retired from teaching,
For married women did not work, it was not done;
However, since once a teacher always a teacher,
I became the star pupil in a class of one.
She vowed that she had never lacked for conversation

Since at the age of eighteen months I learned to speak,
From which time, she swore with pride and exasperation,
    I continued talking what she called "a blue streak".
Our dialogue, uninterrupted for a decade
    Except by the demands of school and sleep and play,
Persisted silently in spite of separation,
    And continues to do so inwardly today,
Unchecked, unedited, uncensored, and uncensured:
    I told her as indeed I owed her everything,
Even or especially when I had been naughty,
    Hoping that confession would draw the guilty sting.
Brought up in a belief in corporal chastisement
    When merited, she would place me over her lap
And reluctantly administer a brisk spanking
    While both of us wept at every half-hearted slap.
Much as I disliked the pain and humiliation,
    What I minded most was the sense of disgrace,
As sinners are said to regret the loss of heaven—
    Her silence and the grim expression on her face,
All the many signs of temporary displeasure
    Which as I grew up came more and more to replace
Most of the grosser forms of physical correction.
    Fortunately my disfavour was always brief,
At least until my mother's ultimate withdrawal
    When guilt was a chief ingredient in my grief.

While the solitary issue on which we differed
    Fundamentally did not urgently arise
Until I was twelve, my troubled, transparent questions
    (I had no secrets from her, and told her no lies)
Shocked this undiagnosed, already dying woman
    Into trying to draw a reasonable line
Between intellectual inquiry and pleasure,
    Which I found in practice difficult to define.
Betrayed without knowing how or why by her body,
    She cannot be blamed for thinking the body bad.
For her day and age comparatively enlightened,
    She did not warn me that I would go blind and mad.
Still, she marched me off to the family physician

Who had treated—lightly—my many childish ills,
   As if there were any remedy for the symptoms
      Of puberty in poultices, potions or pills.
First I had to submit to the humiliating
   Ritual of stripping for a real body search
To sit shivery on the examining table
   With my hands clasped in front of me as if in church
While young Doctor Wilde probed with indelicate queries
   The seat and course of this disquieting disease
Which he pronounced incurable but wholly normal
   With observations meant to put me at my ease,
Couched in a reassuringly man-to-man manner
   But in language more clinical and latinate
Than that habitually in use among schoolchildren,
   Which it took no medical handbook to translate;
However, he wanted to put me on a diet:
   Diagnosis: less oversexed than overweight.
Chilled by a nudity which was neither forbidden
   Nor seductive, I was glad when told to get dressed
While the doctor talked to my mother in his office
   And tried in my regard to set her mind at rest.

On our way home, however, she still seemed worried,
   Less by my moral than her physical decline,
Warned that it was she who had need of the physician
   Whereas I would be better off with the divine.
Frightened, I did not grasp the meaning of this sentence
   At once, but took her hand, or rather she took mine.
There followed further visits, other consultations,
   Till she had to undergo what would be the first
Of several exploratory operations
   From which we feared what we presently learned: the worst.

In and out of hospital, always convalescent,
   Yet never again completely physically well,
For over a year she pitted passive resistance
   Against the active malignancy of a cell.
Outwardly unchanged, as long as I was permitted
   To see her, until a few months before the end,

She kept a moribund eye on my misbehaviour,
    Which by hook or by crook determined to amend,
Against all odds and all by myself I succeeded
    In what was quaintly called, leaving myself alone,
No mean achievement for someone thus twice abandoned,
    With no resources to fall back on but his own.
Nevertheless, contrary to custom and nature,
    Canute-like I stemmed awhile puberty's flood tide.
It was not, I suppose, unlike giving up smoking,
    Though that I could not say because I never tried,
Having spent my potential for self-abnegation
    At an early age, to my undying remorse.
At the time the undeniably final sanction
    Of death lent the maternal prohibition force.
Grief and guilt form an unbeatable combination,
    A natural if dangerously nutty one
Under whose strict, repressive joint administration
    I quit doing that which I had hardly begun.

The sun, I daresay, would not miss an errant planet,
    But a planet cannot survive without its sun,
Unless it becomes its own incandescent focus,
    Or else—something that is not infrequently done
Albeit in contradiction of the laws of physics,
    (And heaven only knows how elastic they are)—
Wander off in search of some bright celestial object
    And go into orbit around another star.
While sorrow cannot imagine the end of sorrow
    Any more than a sleeper dream himself awake,
The first, worst pain must imperceptibly diminish
    Day by day to a dull, domesticated ache.
Enjoined as we are to lay up treasure in heaven,
    Heaven offers little if any interest;
It is in the saving bonds of earthly affection
    That we poor worldly creatures had better invest.
If I repudiated the paternal wisdom
    That would discourage me from mourning overmuch,
In time I forgot life's elementary lesson:
    'It is a dreadful thing to love what death can touch.'

DECEMBER: BOXING DAY

Rattling backwards aboard the so-called interurban,
    (For there were no cities for it to go between,
Only sleepy villages and scattered farm buildings
    Interrupting the empty, snow-bound, rural scene),
With one cheek pressed to the cold, unresponsive window
    As it shivered and shook, my inattentive look
Glazed on the passing, frigidly pastoral landscape,
    My mind in a fog, my forefinger in a book,
Anticipating by a few years the route followed
    Back East when I finally left B.C., alone
In the tram except for a few taciturn locals,
    Not lonely but significantly on my own,
My first independent journey of any distance,
    Imagination raced ahead along the line
As I tried to recognize the name of my station
    In the conductor's incomprehensible whine:
Chilliwack, Abbotsford, Cloverdale, Langley Prairie,
    The whistle stops that modify the proper nouns
Of the Fraser River and its dependent Valley,
    Regularly inflected adjectival towns
Consisting of a single street, a few commercial
    Establishments, feedstore, barber shop and bank,
The established churches, Anglican and United,
    Single-storey facades incuriously blank.
At intervals between these uninviting outposts
    The isolated structures spotted from the train
Were large, scarlet barns with squat mediaeval silos.
    Between the mountains the rich alluvial plain
Was covered with an uncharacteristic carpet,
    Temporary in this temperate clime, of snow,
Which rendered the fertile farmland cold and forbidding.
    At each stop a drab brick or gingerbread depot
Tottered forward to meet the track, while on each platform
    The observant traveller might rarely discern

Bits of those muted, transitory mini-dramas,
    The Joy of Parting or The Sorrow of Return.

I had been invited for a week in the country
    From the day after Christmas, that is Boxing Day,
By Scottish friends of the family, the MacSporrans,
    To see in the New Year, which they called Hogmanay.
They had a son about my age whose name was Randy
    With whom it was assumed that I would want to play.
Newly emigrated from the so-called Old Country,
    The fabled cradle of our race across the sea,
(The origin, at least to judge by nomenclature,
    Of more than half the population of B.C.,
Recalled, like childhood, with sentimental nostalgia,
    In direct proportion to one's removal thence),
They had recently moved anew, from New Westminster
    Where we first knew them, to this rustic residence
Which I had not as yet seen, as live-in caretakers
    Of a large, disused ecclesiastical pile,
Inhabiting the rambling rectory adjacent
    Constructed in the Victorian Gothic style.
But I anticipate the object of my journey—
    It was ever my weakness to anticipate.
The MacSporrans for their part were far from nostalgic
    For whatever it was that made them emigrate.
Randy already had almost lost his Scots accent,
    Though his parents still pulled out all the glottal stops.
The New World, classless, crass and materialistic,
    They thought magnificent, especially the shops.
Not that there were many such in their present rural
    Vicinity; the nearest town was far from near,
Living as they said they did in the midst of nowhere,
    Which locus I noticed with a jolt was now here.

The train shuddered to a halt at a wayside station
    I had recognized as my destination no
Sooner than a snowball exploded on the window,
    Thrown by Randy gesticulating in the snow.

Jumping up, I grabbed my father's World War One kitbag
    And scrambled off, as the conductor shouted " 'board!"
Into range of a wet bombardment by my playmate
    Whom I had distinctly confused feelings toward
As an insensitive yet seductive young yahoo,
    Easy, ignorant, yet not easily ignored.
Reminding myself I had never really liked him
    Very much, with his blooming cheeks and cheeky bloom,
A prickly rose of which the anagram was Eros,
    I greeted him with all the coolness I could assume,
My nonchaloir outwardly unreciprocated,
    To judge by the casual but good-natured cuff
He gave me in greeting, along with a wet handful
    Down my back of rapidly melting cold white stuff.
With a valedictory toot the tram departed
    As Randy, hooting, led me up the forest trail
In pursuit. Steep and slippery, both sides were bordered
    By forbidding tree trunks like the bars of a jail.
Gambolling ahead, my guide cavorted and capered,
    Goat-footed as a satyr on the tricky slope,
Shewing off with the unnecessary bravado
    That branded him both a daredevil and a dope.
Why had I imagined just now that I disliked him,
    When my feelings went deeper, verging on disgust
With his high-spirited, gross and goofy behaviour—
    A distaste that any moment might change to lust?
Disturbing because of my grim determination
    In the wake of my bereavement to remain chaste,
Desire denied, hardly acknowledged, was diverted
    Hypocritically to fastidious distaste.
Unaware of, and indifferent to my scruples,
    Randy disappeared around a bend in the track,
Rushing out when I reached the same turning from ambush,
    An abominable snowman on the attack.
Behind his back I glimpsed a squat gothic church tower
    Instantly obliterated by his onslaught:
It looked as if it had been clumsily translated,
    Like him, from some remote and more historic spot.

Together in a whirl of flailing limbs we tumbled
    Into a snowdrift that looked softer than it felt,
Like an immaculate counterpane rudely rumpled
    By Randy's sneaky incursion below the belt.
Such manoeuvres, permitted in all puerile horseplay,
    Always resisted, rarely went as far as rape;
Among male animals comparable behaviour
    Decides between dominant and submissive ape.
My resistance was not only token but frigid
    To his playful, persistent and glacial advance,
As astride me, giggling something about a "snow-job"
    He thrust a chill fistful down the front of my pants,
Seeing he was wearing a one-piece woolen snow-suit
    And prompted by a desire ostensibly to get
Even, as was dictated by masculine honour,
    I tugged down his zipper and shoved a sopping wet
Mitt in, snatching it back as from an incandescent
    Stove, at the touch and sight of his glowing bare skin.
How often in Autumn have you seen a horse-chestnut's
    Rough husk crack to expose the polished nut within?
Like Snow White and Rose Red, who under the torn bearskin
    Penetrated the enchanted prince's disguise,
Flabbergasted by this unforeseen revelation,
    We gazed at each other in mutual surprise,
As when, last year, exasperated by his antics
    In class, I had stabbed a pen-nib into his palm,
Uncomplaining of such unfair painful mistreatment
    He looked at me with the same speculative calm.
Standing up abruptly—the free-for all was over—
    He quickly zipped up and blundered off up the path.
My ideas needing adjustment like my clothing,
    I followed at leisure repenting my rash wrath.
We saved our breath for the ascent, our conversation
    At the very best of times sporadic and spare,
The spectres of unspoken sentences between us
    Stillborn, mute exhalations on the frigid air.
Looking back where we had lain, I saw two snow angels
    Extending wide their moulting wings beneath the trees,

Like something once wondered at in the Book of Knowledge,
    Monstrous, many-armed, mythical divinities.

Randy's mother greeted us in the open doorway
    Of the shabby, old-fashioned former rectory:
A typical British housewife, frightfully jolly,
    For whom, I presently learned, every meal was tea.
"Just look at the pair of ye," she exclaimed, "Ye're sopping,"
    With a mixture of reproof and anxiety
Lest we catch our death or dirty her spotless lino.
    She packed us off upstairs at once to change our clothes,
Which we did, on my part with modest circumspection,
    On his with Anglo-Saxon attitudes and oaths
Calculated in equal measure to impress me
    With the extent of his development and growth
Since we had seen each other last, an exhibition
    Of his full-fledged manhood, or manliness, or both,
Displayed with the same unblushing enthusiasm
    As a stamp collection or enviable bunch
Of baseball cards . . . Shrugging me off as a wet blanket,
    He sulkily dressed and led the way down to lunch.
The otherwise empty front hall was dominated
    By a large, bedizened idol, the Christmas tree,
Fresh from the forest, hung with homemade decorations
    Its green life truncated for a nativity.
Christmas at home had been treelessly celebrated,
    If that is the word, by my father, as a fete
Worse than death; I was given those practical presents,
    Like long woolen underwear, that all children hate,
As if to signal that I was a child no longer
    To be indulged: a lie I subscribed to, although
I envied Randy less his new racing toboggan
    Than that misleading book, "What Every Boy Should Know".

Luncheon consisted of tea and blueberry pancakes,
    A confection for which I did not greatly care.
It was all I could do to finish my first helping,
    But Randy helpfully ate the rest of my share.

His mother was not my idea of a mother,
    With her brisk cheerfulness and permanent-waved hair,
Nor was his father, who came to table in braces,
    What a father ought to be. A good-tempered bloke,
And like most easy-going folk notably lazy,
    Unlike his energetic wife he seldom spoke.
If the MacSporrans seem caricatures of grown-ups,
    To a child adults are often figures of fun;
Yet Randy's did not look old enough to be parents,
    In my biased and unasked-for opinion.
Nevertheless it was with an air of paternal
    Authority that his father put down his cup
Saying, "Before you young fellows get into mischief,
    Why not work off a little steam by washing up?"

Afterwards in view of the seasonable weather
    Randy suggested a walk, or rather a run,
A chase through the mazy depths of the wintry forest
    In the pale splendour of the brief afternoon sun.
Little tempted by this intemperate excursion,
    I should have preferred to loiter indoors and lounge
In front of the tiny fire which in British fashion
    Was kept barely alive all day in the lounge,
Alone or with a more intelligent companion
    In the rather less strenuous form of a book,
For if Randy could read I seldom saw him open
    Anything more serious than a comic-book.
Teasing me for my sedentary inclinations,
    He insisted that since it was his parents' house,
Whatever my tastes we had to do what he wanted,
    So I submitted as befitted a town mouse.

The landscape was photographically dichromatic,
    The so-called evergreens black as India ink,
The snow in striking contrast white as writing paper,
    Only the sky beginning to be tinged with pink.
Randy, at his age insufficiently selfconscious
    To respect that nature which he seemed to belong
In, cheerfully polluted its beauty and silence

With meaningless ejaculations and rude song:
Rollicking out loud, "Roll Me Over in the Clover"—
    An unseasonable wish at this time of year—
But he carolled all the filthy verses, moreover
    With variations which I would rather not hear.
At first I had assumed that we were going nowhere
    Particular, but soon the object of our stroll
Peeked through a sketchy screen of coniferous branches
    Beneath us as we topped a negligible knoll:
A small farm isolated in a shallow valley,
    Picturesque but squalid, a cluttered rural slum.
"Red's place," Randy conspiratorially pointed
    To the unpainted barn. "He asked if you could come,
He said he'd kind of like to meet a city slicker.
    I bet he's up in the hayloft, sneaking a smoke."
Nobody was visible, not a thing was moving
    Except from one tin chimney a thin thread of smoke.
Distances differ so deceptively in winter
    As arctic explorers discover to their cost
When in their search for the mythical Northwest Passage
    They find nothing beyond the fact that they are lost.

But in a few minutes we slipped into the biggest
    Building of the bunch, which I had identified
As the barn by its size, a characterization
    Confirmed by the animal atmosphere inside.
Here we were greeted with no formal introduction
    Other than the familiar salutation, "Hi!"
By a skinny kid about our age in worn denim
    Overalls, who must be Red. No need to ask why,
He had the milky skin typical of a red-head
    And the expression on his foxy face was sly,
At the same time somehow both innocent and vicious,
    The secret, knowing look of the rustic wise-guy.
Randy rather rudely asked him what he was doing.
    He answered with a rude gesture, Milking the cow,
And challenged us to try, alleging it was easy,
    "All it takes is practice, everybody knows how."
I protested my ignorance. In New Westminster

Nothing bigger than a chicken was to be seen,
While on my old agricultural uncles' model
    Dairy farm they did the dirty work by machine.
Red scoffed, "We don't need any of your new-fangled gadgets
    Here; we do it the good old-fashioned way, by hand."
Blushing unseen in the comforting semi-darkness
    I sat down on a three-legged stool by the grand
Ruminating creature that patiently awaited
    My inept and futile attentions in her stall,
For no matter how I followed Red's rough instructions
    I could not elicit a single drop with all
My pulling, squeezing, rubbing, stroking, yanking, jerking,
    To the vast amusement of Randy and his chum
Who had to support each other, helpless with laughter,
    "What's the matter?" Red taunted, "Can't you make it come?"
Then taking my place beside the poem of pity
    Who was getting fidgetty and switching her tail,
He patted her, and sent a stream of steaming liquid
    Contemptuously cascading into the pail.
Randy, who had already been initiated
    In these manual mysteries, was moved to gloat,
But I stared loftily up at the vaulted ceiling,
    Noting its resemblance to an overturned boat
As well as to much grander gothic architecture,
    A similarity that I found comforting,
Striving to ignore the biological banter
    Which my collusive companions were bandying
Back and forth amid fits of Rabelaisean sniggers,
    Though I doubt they had ever heard of Rabelais,
Who I must admit impressed me in translation
    As no funnier, though much more decent, than they.
Red mischievously directed a jet of milky
    Fluid at me, which spattered the front of my pants,
Reducing Randy and him to puerile hysterics
    At the stain and its sinister significance.
Upset, outraged, and what was worse, slightly excited,
    I took refuge in silent, undignified flight,
Blundering out of the barn's foetid bovine twilight
    Into the inhuman, cold, and oncoming night,

Pursued by an indecent derisory chorus
    Which while diabolical was hardly unkind.
Turning my back on imaginary temptation,
    I still could not erase its image from my mind,
Nor the suspicion of what my tempters were up to
    Perhaps behind my back the moment it was turned,
As like a mirage against the darkening snowscape
    I projected the lively pleasures I had spurned.

I retraced our steps, literally, for the only
    Clue to the route back was our footprints in the snow,
Which I followed like a hunter tracking a wounded
    Animal: myself of an hour or so ago.
A discernible, unambiguously double
    Trail led me up the slope and into the obscure
Wood where I would no longer worry about Randy:
    He knew his way home by heart, of that I was sure;
But I could not stop depicting in technicolour
    The probable upshot of his rude overture.
Although roundabout, the route, like the rowdy frolic
    Which it was the map of, was surprisingly short,
And in no time I saw the bright, uncurtained windows
    Of the vicarage like a snowed-in ski resort.
Reluctant as I was to face his parents' questions
    As to Randy's whereabouts and my own return,
I paused amidst the chilly symbol of my silly
    Determination sooner to freeze than to burn
And like an ascetic mortifying his body
    Rolled, albeit clothed, in the frozen element,
Which had an effect opposite to that intended,
    So I rose and returned, wet, cold, but continent.
That night before bedtime, not long after a supper
    Of finnan haddie, tinned fruit, tea, and sliced white bread,
I departed, to Randy's dumb-struck disappointment,
    From normal practice by not sharing the same bed.
The innocence, or the cynicism, of parents
    Encourages queer bedfellows, often as not,
But Randy's mother, though mildly put out, consented
    In the same room to make up a separate cot.

I hurriedly undressed and put on my pajamas
 With my back turned but not without a furtive glance
At Randy's reflection in the unshaded window
 As he pranced around the room in his underpants.
On my knees beside my makeshift couch, a position
 I adopted every evening now to recite
The Lord's Prayer, I sighed, "Lead us not into temptation,"
 As Randy got into bed and put out the light;
Then, prematurely thankful my prayers had been answered,
 I crawled between the icy sheets and said Good Night,
A wish that was at first received in pregnant silence
 Which proved, however, neither protracted nor deep
Broken in less than a minute by the *pro forma*
 But age-old ritual whisper, "Are you asleep?"
A prelude to more undercover hanky-panky
 Perhaps than maturer opening gambits, such
As a drink or an invitation to view art-work,
 Or "Have you got a match?" or "Do you come here much?"
He followed this up, in the absence of an answer,
 With an apology, or what was meant for one,
"You shouldn't have gone off mad. We were only kidding.
 After you went and left we had a lot of fun.
Red told me to be sure to see you come tomorrow."
 I pretended I had no idea what he meant.
"Remember that time when we were up in your attic. . ?"
 That clumsy and inconclusive experiment
Which I could not deny for I was in no danger
 Of forgetting it, had occurred last year before
Our move, my mother's death and my reform. In horror
 Now I swore, "I don't do things like that any more."
Unabashed, Randy, without attempting to argue
 Snorted and rolled over and soon began to snore.

Exhausted by the Pyrrhic victory of virtue
 With its guerdon of regret and insomnia,
I fell asleep at once and woke surprised by sunlight
 And the wet evidence of a nocturnal thaw,
Unsightly proof of the fickleness of the climate
 In the coastal range of British Columbia.

The view from the bare window no longer resembled
    A rumpled sheet but an untidy patchwork quilt
Strewn with bits of unmelted snow like crumpled kleenex.
    My own deliquescence inspired no little guilt.
I stowed my tell-tale pajamas under the pillow
    When I had dressed, and tiptoed to the bedroom door,
Before noticing that the other bed lay empty,
    Like Randy's undershorts discarded on the floor.

In the bathroom I splashed my face with icy water.
    The house was kept at a British fifty degrees
Fahrenheit which probably reminded the homesick
    Occupants of holidays in the Hebrides.
But when I descended to breakfast I was greeted
    By nobody, the sole sign of my absent hosts
Cold toast in the toast-rack, tepid tea in the teapot.
    I might have been the guest of hospitable ghosts.
Not yet perturbed by their unexplained disappearance
    But incurably curious, I took this chance
For some impromptu solitary exploration,
    An unguided tour of what they called the old manse.
Its decor brought back to me childhood's lost Atlantis,
    That mythical land now irretrievably sunk,
A mix of solid Victorian comfy-cosy
    And flimsy, cheap, uncomfortable modern junk
Owing more to the MacSporrans' straitened finances
    Than to their taste, though that might be equally poor,
But so much roomier than the little apartment
    Which we lived in, crammed with nostalgic furniture.
Some substantial but shabby mahogany pieces
    Which in style and lack of polish displayed their age
Must date from some departed clerical incumbent
    When this furnished house had still been a vicarage.
Two overstuffed chairs and a long-suffering sofa
    Were upholstered in cretonne, or possibly chintz.
The few pictures that vied with the faded wallpaper
    In dulness were sentimental polychrome prints,
In view of their Caledonian subject matter—
    Collies and kilts and quotations from Rabbi Burns—

Icons reminiscent of the MacSporrans' homeland,
  In contrast to a few exotic potted ferns.
Not only were the windows innocent of curtains,
  The dusty floors did not support a single rug;
In the unlived-in living room the open fireplace
  Produced little heat but a perpetual fug.
The apparent absence of any reading matter
  But an incongruous copy of *Country Life*
Explained Randy's sad lack of literary culture;
  But opening a final door like Bluebeard's wife
I found myself in a well-stocked but stuffy study,
  The hideout of some vanished vicar, by its looks,
Its windowless walls hide-bound from floor to ceiling
  With ranks of long-unread and unreadable books
Of a theological stamp, principally sermons
  With here and there a slightly more secular text,
Among which monuments to piety and learning
  My eye alighted on *The Guide to the Perplexed*.
The very thing I was looking for! just the ticket,
  I hoped, to tell me exactly what to do next.
I opened it hopefully, but was disappointed
  To find the knotty perplexities that had vexed
The contemporaries of the Mosaic Rambam
  So remote and inapplicable to myself.
Had no one before experienced my dilemma?
  I sighed as I restored the guidebook to the shelf,
Which I scanned in vain for more titillating titles
  Than *The Christian Year* and *Meditations in Lent*;
Hopes raised by *Apologia Pro Vita Sua*
  Were dashed by *The Apocryphal New Testament*.
Short-sightedly I never expected to enter
  A library where I was not at once at home,
Not the Reading Room of the British Museum
  Nor even the Vatican Library in Rome,
But here for some reason the omnivorous bookworm
  Was unable to find a single tasty tome.
Temporarily disenchanted with the study
  And the conversation of crack-pots, prigs and bores,
Resorting to reserves of natural resources

I wandered outside to explore the damp outdoors.
It was that season when the ancients celebrated
    The birthday victory of the Unconquered Sun
Which we call Christmas; today the annual come-back
    Appeared audibly already to have begun,
As evidenced by the symphonic sound of melting
    And winter lyrically loosening its grip.
Any British Columbian national anthem
    Must orchestrate this syncopated drip drip DRIP.
Ridiculous in its uncultivated setting
    Against a wild background of cedar, pine and birch,
Stood at a little distance from where I was standing
    A large gothic folly in the form of a church.
Built in the last century for a congregation
    That had stubbornly failed to materialize,
Its majestic but melancholy isolation
    Exaggerated its archaic style and size.
This edifice, under the care of Randy's father,
    I assumed would be locked; nevertheless I tried
A side door, which swung open on unctuous hinges,
    And in the twinkling of an eye I was inside.
The interior had the air of a museum
    That is seldom visited, or a long-locked room,
Stately and stale as a disaffected cathedral
    And lifeless as a freshly excavated tomb.
Over pew and pulpit and altar stained-glass windows
    Cast a subaqueous Preraphaelite gloom.
On first peeking into Roman Catholic churches
    I found them, with their statues and the vigil lamp
That signified something described as The Real Presence,
    Cosy and (a word that I did not know yet) camp.
Whereas to set foot in a church except on Sundays
    Seemed to one of my Protestant upbringing odd,
I was here, in the absence of incense and image,
    Appalled by the emptiness of the house of God.
So we may imagine did magnanimous Titus
    Stand aghast when he strode at last, after the fall
Of Jerusalem, into the Holy of Holies,
    And found there nothing whatever but a blank wall

Once he had torn asunder the veil of the temple:
    No idol, no altar, no mystery at all.
In such ascetic indeed aseptic surroundings
    Prayer seems out of place and a waste of time, apart
From the kind of prayer that I had not yet discovered
    For myself, what Blake praised as the practice of art.

Unmemorable, the week of my winter visit
    Passed without outward incident, outside a book,
For I had not made a connection between fiction
    And the facts of life. No wonder if Randy took
Offense at my studied neglect and felt rejected!
    Yet it was not he I studied so hard to snub
Exclusively but the world, the flesh and the devil,
    Plus any other members of the hell-fire club.
The probability of life on other planets
    Sometimes seems no more remote than we do from each
Other: we suspect extraterrestrial beings
    Exist, but hopelessly forever out of reach.
For Randy I felt none of the romantic ardour
    That in the case of Don Wisdom disguised my lust,
Rather an unwilling physical fascination
    Which I succeeded in curbing, but only just.
The former vague attraction in the adult novels
    That I was reading played a respectable part,
While for the latter, all too specific in practice,
    I had found as yet no fictional counterpart.
If his parents were puzzled by this novel coolness
    Between us, they said nothing, perhaps thinking such
Distance due to our having so little in common,
    Whereas from my point of view we had all too much.

New Year's Eve—Hogmanay—was chastely celebrated
    To the inaccurate refrain of Auld Lang Syne
Early, for we were packed off to bed before midnight,
    Randy glumly to his and I gladly to mine.
Earlier, as it was the eve of my departure
    As well, while we were out in the kitchen alone
Washing up the supper dishes, Randy had offered

Me one last chance in a disheartened undertone.
"How about a small private going-away party
     Later, to really send you off in style?
You know you always used to like to—What's the matter?"
     But I shook my head with a superior smile,
In lieu of an apology or explanation
     Complaining unfairly, "Whatever made you think
I was like that?" The rude sound he made in answer
     Resulted when he pulled the plug out of the sink.
How often were my sensibilities affronted
     In those days by some similar disgusting noise,
At the same time grossly offensive and suggestive
     Of the well-known tendency of boys to be boys.
I thanked him for his hospitality, sincerely,
     Suspecting that I should seldom see him again.
In later life I heard he had become a Mountie,
     Going to show they do not always get their men.

I mounted the stairs to bed for the last time rather
     Like one condemned than, as I thought, like one reprieved.
Self-condemned, how could I ever commute my sentence?
     Self-defeated yet self-righteous, relieved yet grieved.
Next morning in my old kit bag beside my troubles
     I packed up the library books that I had read
That week, my unpaid, true, entertaining companions:
     Wuthering Heights, Bleak House, The Naked and the Dead.
My appetite, indiscriminately voracious,
     Thus tasteless, devoured anything that had a plot
As a means of escape, for in my observation
     This was one thing that ordinary life had not.

JANUARY: EPIPHANY

To such overtures, with their theme and variations,
    I remained obdurately tone-deaf as a boy,
Only later scoring in serial arrangements
    That which I was no longer able to enjoy.
Upright, or uptight? What difference does one letter
    Make? All the difference in the world! *Voluntas*
Being a misleading Mediaeval misreading
    Of Virgil's Sua quemque trahit voluptas,
Where the piffling distinction between will and pleasure
    Appears as glaring and profound as day and night.
Yet it must be granted that in practice the upright
    All too often prove normally uptight,
A term which had not yet been coined, or counterfeited,
    At the time in question, any more than 'turned on',
Both neologisms that form useful additions
    To a living language's loose-leaf lexicon.

Love rejected, elementary, kindergarten
    Love, exacts fantastic revenge in retrospect,
When too late one guesses the value of the very
    Advances one was backward enough to reject.
Those things that we have not done have a mythic status
    Superior to anything that we have done.
Most of mankind's matter of fact, well-documented
    Mistakes are unimportant in comparison
With something that probably never really happened
    Like the Incarnation, a fictional event
That has transformed more human lives for worse or better
    Than any merely historical incident.
So the seminal accidents of adolescence
    Which may never have occurred, as often as not,
Stand out in bold relief only decades thereafter
    And root and flower if at all in afterthought.
The wistful pleasures of the preterite subjunctive
    Assuage the pains of the present indicative;

In actuality we live between the perfect
    Tense and some timeless eternal imperative.
Anyone who patronizes the past is foolish.
    To all those whose native speech is Now, Then is Greek.
Already my tantalizing stay in the country
    Seemed to have lasted rather longer than a week,
And yet to have blurred and shrunk, as within a crystal
    Paperweight the miniscule landscape if one shakes
It, is obscured by a blizzard of opalescent
    Infinitesimal artificial snowflakes.

I returned to school less than normally reluctant.
    Widely advertised as an antidote for grief,
The daily routine of the curriculum provided
    Emotional support, distraction, and relief.
As an elementary school underachiever
    I was astonished to see my name at the top
When the results of the mid-year exams were posted,
    In everything, that is, except Phys. Ed. and Shop.
In proportion as our studies acquired real content,
    My academic appetite, so long suppressed,
Revived: English, Math and French, even Social Studies
    All took on an unprecedented interest.
My scholastic career so far was a disaster.
    I began at a disadvantage, long ago
Having learned to read, I was by successive teachers
    Unsuccessfully discouraged from doing so.
Having taught myself to write on our old typewriter,
    I could see no point in flowing copperplate
Inculcated by something called the MacLean's Method,
    Which they tried in vain to get me to imitate.
Nor was I quick to grasp alphabetical order,
    (For I had phonetically first guessed how to spell,
To the dismay of those semiliterate spinsters
    Who made primary school a propaideutic hell),
Till I was compelled to consult a dictionary,
    Card-catalogue or telephone directory.
The still prevalent view of early education
    As a kind of occupational therapy

Argues an Augustinian concept of childhood
    As intractable and inherently depraved,
Which made many old maids baby-sitters or gaolers
    Whose little charges always, of course, misbehaved.
The obvious purpose of this repressive system
    Was to teach us if nothing else how to know our place
In the social structure, a pyramid consisting
    In Canada almost entirely of a broad base.
Cheerful obedience, mute duty and decorum,
    Pointless industry and unquestioning respect:
The conformist virtues emphasized in the classroom
    Were all my young countrymen were taught to expect
From life. To reinforce the taboo against talking
    In class, we were told to emulate an old bird
Proverbial for taciturnity, the hoot-owl
    Whose lesson was, "The less he spoke the more he heard."
Dismissing all birds as not only dumb but stupid,
    I hooted at this propaganda as absurd,
But could not avoid acquiring the well-bred whisper
    So characteristic of all Canadians,
Incapable of raising their voices in public
    Like loud-mouthed Britons and louder Americans.

Penmanship and anthropomorphic nature study
    Prevented me from learning much till Seventh Grade,
When I stumbled on another kind of writing
    And found in nature more than a cute masquerade.
One Spring day before the commencement of this story
    Some boys had taken off their shirts while playing ball
In the playground, when our Grade Six teacher, Old Lady
    Hannah, seeing them, threw up a window to bawl
Them out for indecency, calling them "half-naked"
    In horrified accents, while I raised a cheap laugh
And earned a dirty look and the threat of chastisement
    By asking whether it did not matter which half?
This eldritch woman was an exacting task-mistress,
    And like many of her profession taught by rote,
Writing out our lessons in long-hand on the blackboard
    And making us copy exactly what she wrote;

These copies she then laboriously corrected,
     Not for content—there was little enough of that—
But for fidelity to her dotty handwriting:
     Perfect training for a forger or copycat.
In Junior High School the jejune misinformation
     On the board became diagrams and paradigms,
And while I was constantly chided for my hen-tracks,
     Untidiness was no longer the worst of crimes.
Less bored, I soon found my footing and a new standing
     In subjects like English, French and Geometry,
But in some areas not covered in the classroom
     I remained woefully and wilfully at sea.
With the other underprivileged in the lunchroom,
     A classroom set aside for those who brought their lunch
When it was too wet to go outside, I consorted
     Perforce. They were an ill-behaved and foul-mouthed bunch,
Who since the sexes at noon hour were segregated
     As if there were something salacious about food,
Indulged in bare-faced badinage and brazen antics
     At once incongruously innocent and lewd.
I have never since heard and seldom read such language
     As what spewed from the lips of nearly beardless boys.
On rainy days pandemonium in the lunchroom
     Prevailed, and not only because of all the noise.
Meanwhile I, silent and shy with mortification,
     Tried to hide my blushes in a library book;
During priapic pantomimes with a banana
     It was harder not to listen than not to look.
Don Wisdom of course was among the lucky many
     Who went home for lunch, as I had been glad to do
Before the fatal illness and death of my mother,
     When willy-nilly I joined the unhappy few,
Among whom I made one sad, happenstance companion:
     Neither one of us ever suggested we meet
Elsewhere, for like castaways or starving survivors
     All we could talk about was what we liked to eat.
He had first sidled up to me during a ballgame
     To propose a reciprocal relationship
To which I replied with a current vulgarism

In keeping with his vulgarity, "I'm not hip."
Thereafter into our gastronomic discussions
　　Over stale sandwiches he liked to introduce
Allusions to equally stale but always juicy
　　Gossip concerning the drawbacks of self-abuse,
Which he inveighed against with a smug disapproval
　　I found reassuring despite his bona fide
Jansenist resignation to the predetermined
　　Inevitability of what he decried.
He dwelt with justified relish upon the certain
　　Eventual damnation of the self-satisfied,
Nor do I believe that he believed for a minute
　　All my protestations of total abstinence,
Claiming as he did to deduce the guilty secrets
　　Of our classmates from the flimsiest evidence.
"Boy!" he would asseverate of some blameless cherub,
　　"He must do it a lot! You can tell at a glance
From the way he can't look you in the eye, his stammer,
　　Not to mention that tell-tale stain on his pants."
Not otherwise I picture grubby little devils
　　Whiling away time—eternity—in hell
Till, (as noon hour and school itself were purgatory
　　Like puberty), released by an electric bell.

If beneath the friendless skies of that January
　　My feelings congealed, this was not unnatural,
Living as I did in suspended animation,
　　Whereof lunchtime seemed the symbolic interval,
Going through the clockwork, unemotional motions
　　Of daily life, getting up and going to bed
On time, doing my homework and attending classes
　　Inattentively while at the same time I read
Everything almost I could get hold of in English,
　　My scope still limited by the language I spoke,
As for this baffled and unhappy adolescent
　　Literature became more addictive than Coke.
Young as I was I already appreciated
　　That the worth of a work as a means of escape

Depends on the inexperience of the reader
    For whom the world wears a naively novel shape.
Emily Dickinson could call a book a frigate
    Precisely because she had never seen the sea.
At that early age the most realistic fiction
    Found an ideal, wide-eyed consumer in me;
The genres that disgusted me as too familiar
    Were fairy tales, science fiction, and fantasy.
Fortunately this was before the fad for Tolkien
    In whose prepubescent Fellowship of the Ring
The good and the evil appear equally sexless,
    And death mysteriously to have lost its sting.
However, the wide-spread moralistic objection
    To escapist trash I have never understood;
Nothing affording even momentary comfort
    In our misery could be anything but good.
Studs Lonigan and Anna Karenina offered
    Less complete relief than an undistinguished work
Of which I have forgotten both title and author
    Describing three cheery career girls in New York
In whose sunnily hygienic high-rise existence
    There was no problem common sense could not set right.
This view of life as a Sit. Com. without a laugh track
    Would be arguable if it did not exclude
The facts thereof, which into the most expurgated
    Publications do tend nastily to obtrude:
Why, the namby-pamby National Geographic
    Sometimes exhibited savages in the nude!
That winter it seemed my major preoccupation
    Was the search for something that would not bring a blush
To my just-shaved cheek; but not even Little Women
    Was spotless enough, nor Little Dorrit, nor Flush.
Best sellers like The Robe or Kristin Lavransdatter
    Were as bad as Shakespeare, for Hamlet and MacBeth
Though bowdlerized, inculcated the tragic lesson
    That one inevitable fact of life is death.
Thus the world that was my imaginary oyster,
    Still unopened, was prematurely spoiled for me,

As in a stupid misreading, by intimations
    Of mortality and of immorality.

I found my heterogeneous reading matter
    On the shelves of the public library nearby,
Besides bound classics and Book-of-the-Month Club Selections.
    All that our domestic bookcases could supply,
And I shall write at further length in future chapters
    Of the conflicting information that I gleaned
There outside books: the false, from a virtuous woman,
    The true, from a man whom many would call a fiend.
My early defection from the juvenile section
    Prompted the childrens' librarian to predict
Dementia praecox, but I pursued my ruin
    Undeterred by her fussy would-be interdict.
Yet this same censorious spinster had encouraged
    My debut as an author of the puppet plays,
Ali Baba, Hansel and Gretel, Cinderella,
    Performed by us children during the holidays
On a stage a yard wide in the library basement,
    With home-made marionettes and hand-painted scenes,
For which I wrote my first dramatic adaptations
    Of borrowed plots—but so were Shakespeare's and Racine's.

Constructed on a modest Palladian model,
    Situated in a pocket-handkerchief-sized
Park, architecturally the library building
    Had more class than I or anyone realized
Back then, representing a classical tradition
    That no one I knew particularly prized—
Indeed man-made beauty of any kind was something
    The natives of British Columbia despised.
I write in the past tense, not just because narration
    Of its nature necessarily treats the past
But since the unpretending structure of my childhood
    Had been replaced by a modern eyesore the last
I heard. Novelty reigns supreme in New Westminster
    Where, had she sat there, the Mother of Parliaments
Would long ago have been razed in the name of progress

In favour of something flashy, at great expense.
B.C., naturally endowed with the most splendid
 Unspoiled scenery that the lens has ever seen,
Must be styled an aesthetic wilderness, however
 Indifferent to that fact I was at thirteen.
My sensibility, predominantly verbal,
 Was not so much obtuse as totally untrained.
What drew me to the library was not its handsome
 Facade, but the volumes of wisdom it contained.
Inside, on either side of a central rotunda
 Surmounted by a small verdigris Romanesque
Dome, the various subsidiary departments
 Surrounded the circular circulation desk.
Alphabetically ranked, biography and fiction
 Occupied the library's upfront public part,
Around whose perimeter unobtrusive alcoves
 Held small caches of music, poetry, and art,
With juvenile and reference, the whole collection
 Apart from certain items that were kept apart.
It was on the open shelves that I did my browsing,
 Rarely straying into the sheltered high-brow bays.
Poetry was something I had been taught to laugh at
 At school, where it was often confounded with praise.
Art I despised as compulsory free expression,
 Music I practiced, but without pleasure or skill.
Ignorantly drawn to the kind of education
 Rousseau imagined for that little prig Emile,
I thought that the young should be left to range at random
 Through the world of letters and spell it for themselves.
Certainly I knew I learned much less in the classroom
 Than cruising the open public library shelves.

My intelligence, such as it was, once awakened
 By the word, was not much inclined to speechless awe.
Although I apprehended music as a language
 Half-comprehensible, like French or Algebra,
I did not at once grasp the semantic potential
 Apparent to cavemen, of the pictograph,
Not merely as having minimal graphic talent,

But because Art as it was taught us was a laugh.
The teacher, herself artistic, or rather arty,
    With her musical earrings, clunky beads and quaint
Clothes that looked as if they were stitched out of old curtains,
    Spent her vacations in search of subjects to paint
In picturesque, i.e. poverty-stricken countries
    Whose squalour scads of impasto failed to disguise.
No doubt it was this addiction of hers to foreign
    Parts that dictated our initial exercise,
The confection of implausible travel posters
    In poster paints, which she pretentiously called gouache.
Mine, an imaginary tropical island
    Impressionistically daubed in a muddy wash,
Earned me a deserved if sarcastic E for Effort,
    But not, as it might have done in grade school, a slap.
After Christmas suddenly another instructor
    Took over, a likeable if unlikely chap,
(Male teachers were a novel feature of Grade Seven),
    Who also taught manual arts, hygiene and gym,
All the mysteries in which I was least proficient,
    Drawing no better than I could chisel or swim.
Concerning the fate of his flakey predecessor
    There was no explanation, but rumour ran rife;
I liked to picture her in some Mexican hoosegow
    For misrepresentation with a palette knife.
No amateur of the colourful and exotic
    But influenced by what Attic notions, who knows?
Mr. Manley transformed Art Class into a Life Class
    Persuading some of the more forward boys to pose
Clad in gym trunks, bathing suits, underpants or jockstraps,
    To the covert admiration and overt glee
Of their fellows, often as not studies in scarlet,
    Blushing all over, or as far as one could see.
On one occasion, when the model was Don Wisdom
    (Resolved to demur, I was not so much as asked),
He stood like a statue, unmoving and unmoved by
    The adulation and envy in which he basked.
Like James when he saw, "Divested of every garment
    'Life' on a pedestal and in an attitude,"

I laid down my pencil, lost in dumb contemplation
    Of the perfection of Wisdom practically nude.

My despair of ever being able to capture
    Such perfection on paper had a parallel
In my inability to perform the music
    I admired but had mastered no instrument well
Enough to reproduce, until I found the only
    Discipline at which I could pretend to excell.
My perfunctory private musical instruction
    Had been taken in hand hopefully but too late
When I was given a cheap second-hand piano—
    Just what I always wanted—at the age of eight.
Appropriately my mother was my first teacher,
    For a musician's mother ought to be a muse.
Better suited to the keyboard of a typewriter,
    Which I had taught myself haphazardly to use,
I was woefully deficient in execution
    On either, lacking digital dexterity.
Quick to read anything, I mastered the notation,
    But could not rattle off a simple scale in key.
Mother's patience and musicianship soon exhausted,
    A succession of ill-paid females took her place,
But pianistically my Gradus ad Parnassum,
    Like my fingering, proceeded at a snail's pace.
For one thing I was strangely troubled by the presence
    Beside me on the bench, which horror feminae
(Which I did not comprehend), made me play more badly
    During a lesson than when practicing by my
Self at home; for another, the icky set pieces
    I was expected to perfect and get by heart,
Though all my little skill and fingers could encompass,
    Plainly left a great deal to be desired as art.
I marked time, until my ultimate music teacher,
    A motherly Englishwoman with a moustache,
Declaring that I should never make a pianist,
    Taught me to analyze a fugue by J. S. Bach.
Soon after theory thus superseded practise
    My father, suspicious now he could not hear

My dubious progress, discontinued my lessons,
　　Mercifully cutting short my keyboard career—
A catastrophe for which my teacher consoled me
　　Following her last lesson, on diminished thirds,
Predicting that, in expertness of execution,
　　My chosen medium would be not notes but words.
Prophetic but, unlike most professional prophets,
　　Perceptive, she put her finger on my innate
Calling, which hours of so-called vocational training
　　Had failed to elicit any sign of to date.
From the time I learned how to write of course I had written
　　This and that, short stories, limericks, puppet plays
Unpolished production proportionate to my stature,
　　For I was short-winded—on paper—in those days.
I took it for granted that I should be an author
　　When I grew up, as well as more strenuous things
Like an archaeologist or arctic explorer
　　Or some kind of virtuoso, imaginings
Where I failed to distinguish the opera singer
　　Who pens his memoirs from the pen-pusher who sings.
I devoured the lives of ballerinas and divas
　　Whose performances I could not hope to attend,
Though I listened to the Metropolitan broadcasts
　　Every Saturday morning after "Let's Pretend".
My father would not have countenanced dancing lessons—
　　My lack of agility was a standing joke—
But grudgingly agreed to let me study singing
　　Briefly, before my untrustworthy treble broke.
My voice coach, the local Church of England choir mistress,
　　A native like me of British Columbia,
Seemed more British than any immigrant from Blighty,
　　Almost as Olde Worlde as Victoria,
The provincial capital, a tourist by-word
　　For false imperial notes, tea and la-di-da.
Anglophilia is a common affectation
　　In Canada, but her fondness for little boys,
Proverbial among others of her persuasion,
　　Must have been tested when one made a dreadful noise
As I did in the midst of the Bluebells of Scotland;

But instead of a scolding, from the bric-a-brac
Cluttering her house she gave me a small object
    Of virtue, which mother insisted I give back,
As a consolation prize for my lack of talent
    The kindness of a childless woman, I suppose,
But the end of my vocal hopes marks the beginning
    Of my haphazard collecting of bibelots.
Let me record my benefactress' name: Miss Moffett
    Has no need, unlike others, of a pseudonym
Now that without doubt to their everlasting profit
    She is instructing in solfège the cherubim.

My musical prospects, like so many illusions,
    Did not survive the arrival of puberty,
When my hopes of soloing in The Holy City
    Were shattered, at least in the original key.
While every age has been called an age of transition,
    This was one of transposition, to tell the truth,
Though thanks to a balanced diet and healthy habits
    I had few of the skin-deep eruptions of youth.
Remarkably, while my youthful enthusiasm
    For opera survived the awkward circumstance
Of glandular change, the very first performance
    I attended disenchanted me with the dance
As a pointless kind of prettified callisthenics;
    Furthermore my mature aversion to ballet
Owed much to its accompaniment, thumping music
    By Minkus, Delibes, Adam, Copland and Grofé.
In the same way, my interest in exploration
    At puberty shrunk to a more intimate sphere.
The imagined magnitude of the world in childhood,
    In memory how petty it came to appear!
As reported in the National Geographic
    There were no further unknown regions to explore,
At least on earth. How many far-flung expeditions
    Have arrived to find that Kilroy was there before?
As chimerical vocations evaporated
    Like lost wax, my true bent did not at once stand out.
My father, who saw me as a doctor or a lawyer,

Regarded writing as a waste of time, no doubt.
My mother, when last I saw her as she lay dying,
    Concerning a future she would not see, expressed
Only the hope that I should not 'give up my music',
    And in my own way I have honoured that request.
Far from a harmless pastime or pleasant sideline
    My kind of music, which is going out of style,
Has proved the one thing I am capable of making
    Well enough that all this thankless work seems worthwhile.

My gift arrived during Music Appreciation
    Class, which was treated as a Study Period
By one and all at school, for catching up on homework,
    Forty winks, or masticating the mental cud
While supposedly listening to an example
    Of polyphony by Palestrina, the motet
For Epiphany, Quod Erat Demondstrandum—
    It arrived, but I have not quite unwrapped it yet.
Stamped with the authenticity of a revelation
    And posted, though I did not know it, C.O.D.,
Gratuitous as an unasked-for obligation,
    It came unforseen as any epiphany.
On a blank, lined page of my open loose-leaf notebook
    In pencil in a sprawling illegible hand
I began scrawling, as if taking down dictation,
    Vocables I could not begin to understand.
Till afterwards; nor can I tell how long it lasted,
    This sudden, productive but uncritical trance,
But as the Faber stumbled on faster and faster
    Across the paper the lines were starting to dance.
I know that I did not stop when the record stuttered
    To its conclusion on the cranky gramophone
Or during the teacher's redundant commentary,
    But wrote on regardless of his didactic drone,
No doubt on his favourite theme of Programme Music
    Which was thought to recommend itself to the young
Who mistake all music for onomatopoiea,
    Though I who, however poorly, had played and sung,
Knew better: not so much descriptive as expressive,

The muses speak to us in an archaic tongue.
So when I came to scrutinize what I had scribbled,
    (Which with all my juvenilia was destroyed,
Hence the vain elaboration of these pages
    In a desperate, late attempt to fill the void),
I soon noticed that like much automatic writing
    It fell into the rhythmic cadence of free verse,
As repetitive, rhetorical and long-winded
    As Whitman, the Old Testament, or St.-John Perse.
Spontaneous and derivative, this effusion
    Of feeling it is just as well I cannot quote.
Metre was my metier, but in the beginning
    I wrote poetry without knowing what I wrote:
A dithyramb, or a threnody for my mother?
    An elegy, or an ode to the life to come?
Already I sensed that the subject did not matter
    As much as the beauty of the encomium.

FEBRUARY: VALENTINE'S DAY

I have often idly wondered if one would ever
    Have written unless one had previously read?
The principle of literary imitation
    If not the practice nowadays seems stone cold dead,
At least according to Creative Writing Students
    Whose studious disregard of the printed page
Brands reading as a lowly kind of mass consumption
    In which an inspired word-spinner need not engage.
Fortunately no courses in Creative Writing
    Were elective then at Lord Lovat Junior High,
When what I conceived as poetry in the classroom
    I wrote without encouragement and on the sly,
My only tutors those extenuated volumes
    Perused undercover, as if it were a crime,
Little dreaming (or did I have a premonition?),
    That this skinny novice in the fulness of time
Would become the plump author of so many slender
    Tomes of well-fashioned if unfashionable rhyme,
While in a spirit of eclectic emulation
    I wrote sonnets, sestinas, ballades and rondeaux,
Even had a fling at free verse, on the side, meanwhile
    Doing my academic assignments in prose.
Poetry or what used to pass for it in English
    With rare exceptions excited my interest
Less than what I disinterred on my own, however
    I always managed to get it up for a test,
In part as it was presented as vague abstractions
    Inexplicably expressed in out-of-the-way
Terms: that Poetry is not written with ideas
    I discovered before I discovered Mallarmé.
(If the present work seems a wordy contradiction
    To this rule, my muse is less doctrinaire today.)
Anyway I resolved, and kept my resolution,
    Never again to take a literature course
In my native language, when I could choose, in college,

Among French and Latin, Greek, German, and Old Norse,
In any of which as in a distorting mirror
  The idiosyncrasies of our idiom
May be seen in perspective; except as a hobby,
  The formal study of English struck me as dumb,
As it obviously did my masculine classmates
  Whose major problem in class was staying awake
During discussion of such soporific classics
  As that sedative pill The Lady of the Lake,
Which whatever its depths is badly calculated
  To charm an adolescent sensibility.
I pretended to be amused when Wisdom giggled
  At the witless, unoriginal parody
That went the rounds. Other, less equivocal titles
  Having slipped through the reticule of memory,
Who could ever overlook The Seats of the Mighty
  Or The Lay of the Last Minstrel, subjects of jest
Among those who in The Intermediate Reader
  Relished the sanguinary border ballads best?
Perversely, of all the blood-thirsty plays of Shakespeare,
  The least suitable, Romeo and Juliet,
Hand-picked for young persons, most of whom were not ready
  For heterosexual dalliance quite yet,
Prompted innumerable falsetto renditions
  Of the overly familiar balcony scene,
Which the Bard, accustomed as he was to boy actors,
  Might have approved, but I found obscurely obscene.
For whatever reason, I was never a barmy
  Bardolater, sensibly preferring Racine,
Which may explain why I am writing in a metre
  So alien to English, the Alexandrine,
Instead of a hackneyed domesticated rhythm
  Like unrhymed iambic pentameter or blank
Verse, measured in feet. For this imported metric
  System I have Shakespeare and company to thank.

But lyric poetry, if not purely romantic,
  Had achieved its high-water mark, so we were taught,
During what was known as The Romantic Revival,

Though no one ever explained, revival of what?
These sacred texts with their prosaic commentaries
    Failed to excercise their magic, to be exact
(Which their authors seldom were), on imaginations
    Privately preoccupied by a profane act.
I suspected that in all likelihood our teacher
    Liked those Odes, to the West Wind or a Grecian Urn,
No more than the average, indifferent pupil;
    But one was not there to like, one was there to learn,
Understood as uncritical assimilation
    Of general propositions in paraphrase
Which flouted the basic Romantic proposition
    Engraved in Blake, that the study of art is praise.
The Romantic abstraction par excellence, Nature
    Had for me a soppy, suspect, sinister ring
Since grade school: a dangerous, all-embracing concept
    Manipulated to mean almost anything.
Put off by these nauseous, sentimental glosses,
    I hated to see such splendid texts misconstrued,
Their eccentric design and complex verbal texture
    Reduced to an unpalatable platitude.
Taste being subjective, like natural selection,
    To that extent the analphabet young are right:
Reading can never be a purely passive pastime
    To those whose ambition is learning how to write.
If there was no lesson for me in the Romantics,
    A whole correspondence course in the school of night
Was taught by the symbolists and Elizabethans
    Through the mediumship of T.S. Eliot.
If anyone cared to question my understanding,
    I answered smartly that understanding was not
As important for poetic appreciation
    As the educational establishment thought.
Indisputably the aging modernist masters
    Owed their long-standing contemporaneity
To their being excluded from the approved textbooks,
    Which made them as it were my private property.
Taken in as I was by the spurious glamour
    Attached nowadays to the notion of the new,

In these forerunners of my father's generation
    I found my true contemporaries, whom I knew
Better than any nebish chronological neighbour.
    The movement that had begun with breaking all moulds
Decades earlier, as permanent revolution,
    Seemed to appeal to few other thirteen-year olds.
If I put behind me the formal exercises
    That had stretched to the limit my juvenile skill
In favour of tame experimental excesses,
    Free verse seemed a smashing expression of free will,
At that age. I got the virus out of my system
    Young enough that it did me no permanent harm;
Early innovation like an inoculation
    Immunized me against fashion's infectious charm.

Initially, then, beguiled by the spacey lay-out
    Of most up-to-date publications on the page,
I tried composing directly on the typewriter
    During this imitative, innovative stage.
But the subtle influence of poetic licence
    Proved as insidious for better or for worse
As advertised. My moral standards were perverted
    Quite by A Little Treasury of Modern Verse.
At first it must have seemed strictly coincidental
    This insensible relaxation of my guard,
But virtue appeared ever more reactionary
    As vice enrolled in the ranks of the avantgarde.
While once I found free verse ridiculously easy,
    Now I know that it is astonishingly hard.
Rhyme and metre give the writer more than the reader
    Something to cling to, the line as a kind of guy
Whereby the paragraph is turned into a strophe. . .
    Another modernist fad, the lower case i,
An affectation or psychological symptom
    I for one was not personally tempted by.
For the nonce without rhyme or reason I resisted
    The self-indulgence to which I must soon succumb,
In the liberties of my literary practice
    Refusing to see the libertinage to come.

81

My new activity remained secretive, almost
    Shameful, as I had nobody to whom to show
My output: if my teachers were unsympathetic,
    My father was rather more outspokenly so.
From my age-mates I expected only derision,
    Dreading the sneer of my unacknowledged love,
Whom for a season I scrupulously avoided
    Like that which he was the blameless occasion of.
My recent bereavement had made me the sad object
    Of suspicious commiseration; to my peers,
As to all members of a stiff-upper-lipped culture,
    There was something morbid and sissified in tears.
Beginning as I did in grievous isolation,
    I have continued the same practice to this day;
Notwithstanding the chance of future publication,
    Writing remains a kind of solitary play.

One darkling afternoon in dreary February
    I was waiting to check out some library books
At the circulation desk. I was braced to weather
    A new librarian's questions and searching looks,
But a cultivated, melancholy and gentle
    Strange voice, lady-like, of indeterminate age,
Commented not censoriously on my reading
    Habits, for once without a hint of patronage.
My taste was not so much catholic as eclectic
    In those days; but she did not treat me as a child.
Commending me on my choice of *Lord Weary's Castle*,
    Which I wanted to borrow, she knowingly smiled.
(Less impressed with his half-baked faith than hard-boiled diction,
    I could not, any better than Lowell, foresee
How quickly the gifted but disappointing author
    Would reverse the normal order from *cru* to *cuit*.)
I smiled back at a small, plain, pleasant-looking woman
    Dressed and coiffed with the severity of a nun
Even to the cross on her nonexistent bosom,
    Like my idea of Emily Dickinson.
She glanced down demurely while trying to decipher
    The name on my library card in black and white

But upside down, her own in relief was emblazoned
    On the wooden name plate in front of her: B. Knight.
As she handed me my books she said rather archly
    "So you're our infant literary prodigy?"
A slightly ambiguous, invidious label
    She seemed to apply without any irony,
According me at the same time the adult status
    Stamped on my borrower's card, while I in return
Granted her the kind of grave and grateful attention
    That grown-ups as a rule do too little to earn.
She never exclaimed in astonishment or horror
    Over my latest literary find, "What next?"
But, vetting the books I took out, like an inspector
    Of customs, sometimes shook her head as if perplexed.
As Miss Knight was usually on daytime duty
    Afternoons after school, we soon became fast friends
Of a sort, my first experience of a friendship
    In which means figured more decisively than ends,
The means being our common interest in writing
    (She wasted no time asking if I wrote, and what),
As opposed to a mutual need for each other,
    Though she may have felt more for me than I then thought.
Our acquaintance provoked much amused disapproval
    Among the celibate female library staff,
Ironically, our open association
    Being if anything too innocent by half.
Nevertheless I wish there were some brighter coinage
    Than this whereby her kindness might be reimbursed;
Though I should find other, wiser and better mentors
    In the years to come, Miss Knight was among the first.
In future it would seem as if most of my closest
    Friends were a decade senior on the average,
A gap more impressive in early adolescence
    Than now, when differences diminish with age.
Soon I was showing Miss Knight my juvenile poems
    For critical approbation, at her request,
Only to be for all of her kind words, discouraged
    That she liked the earliest formal ones the best,
Significantly an alliterative ballad

On the maudlin topic of Mary Magdalene,
Already scoffed at as a youthful archaism,
    In which the saint's name constituted the refrain.
However, she made no pretense to be objective,
    But, a fervent indeed fanatical R.C.,
Prized poetry primarily as propaganda
    Fidē, and praised propaganda as poetry.
To her transparent efforts toward my conversion
    I responded not unfavourably, and soon
In a gesture unprecedented from a grown-up
    She asked me to her flat for tea one afternoon.
Appreciating the occasion as a milestone
    (Though I was uncertain along what sacred way)
I gulped when after I had gobbled the last crumpet
    She hauled out her beads and suggested that we pray.

One Friday my father returned the invitation
    On my behalf, naturally anxious to meet
Someone of whom I spoke so highly and so often,
    But was offended when she refused to eat meat.
Thus this auspicious overture was a disaster,
    It would not be easy to decide through whose fault;
I had known nothing of the carnal prohibition;
    Fraser had, and treated it with a grain of salt,
Intolerant of all outlandish superstitions
    While taking for granted those in which he was bred,
Not from high-minded sceptical empiricism
    But an obtuseness of the heart and of the head.
Yet friendship flourished in the face of disapproval.
    How many rewarding relationships since then
Have I not embarked on with sympathetic women,
    So much more approachable than most boys and men!
Still our difference in age and status dictated
    That I never call Miss Knight by her Christian name,
Which I guessed to be Beatrice from her initial.
    In nomenclature, schoolboy practice was the same.
I confessed my immaculate infatuation
    (Supposing confession a feature of her Church)
But her shocked reaction to my annunciation

Concerning Don Wisdom did as much to besmirch
My pure and apparently pointless admiration
    As any rumour a coarse classmate might have spread;
When she asked, had we done 'anything bad together',
    Abashed and bewildered, I had to shake my head.
I could hardly pretend that I had no idea
    Of whatever she suspected us to have done,
But outside of dreams my love found its unique outlet
    In gazing as if dazzled at a far-off sun.
My experiences in the country at Christmas,
    Or rather my rejection of experience,
Like the innuendoes overheard in the lunchroom,
    Had barely scratched the veneer of my innocence.
Furthermore, I could not imagine a connection
    Between the unfeeling propositions I spurned
And the sentimentally idealized idol
    For whom with a pure and taciturn flame I burned.
Needless to say, I was no stranger to temptation,
    With which I wrestled heroically day and night,
Too often feeling the effect of prohibition
    Itself to excite an illicit appetite.

Under the guise of my redundant reformation,
    By means of an encouragement absent at home,
Miss Knight engaged in my spiritual seduction,
    Not to heterosexuality, but Rome.
She gave me a rosary and a Roman missal
    With a saccharine holy card to mark my place,
And a work of literary apologetics
    By a Jesuit, *Fiction as a Means of Grace*,
Undertaking, herself, my religious instruction
    Singlehanded, with more than missionary zeal.
In those days before the Second Vatican Council
    The Church still had a certain aesthetic appeal
For those nurtured in a less flamboyant tradition:
    The incense, the candles, the Latin of the Mass,
Which now in the vernacular has all the magic
    Of an unsatisfactory Sunday-school class.
My father's uninformed anti-catholicism

85

I dismissed as an irrational prejudice,
Uneasily aware of more reasoned criticisms
    Of the faith which were more difficult to dismiss.
A born believer, uninterested in dogma,
    All I asked of the Church Militant was a shield
Against all imaginable carnal temptation
    To which I had promised myself never to yield,
In short a sort of fool-proof moral prophylactic
    (The only kind the barque of Peter would dispense)
Which the more secular religion of my childhood
    Could not sanction, for all its worldly commonsense.

The asseveration, that Catholics are liars,
    Indignantly denied in my credulous youth,
Still describes all believers, in whom I detected
    No more than a nodding acquaintance with the truth
Unless formally promulgated ex cathedra,
    Which only the grossest whoppers are as a rule.
No wonder I was fascinated, shocked, and puzzled
    By the rambunctious gang from parochial school,
A scandalous, therefore glamorous bunch of rowdies
    Whose behaviour was the opposite of strait-laced,
To judge by their reputation and conversation,
    Which were profane, irreverent, and far from chaste.
When I complained of the unedifying conduct
    Of her co-religionists, "Unlike most of those
Born in the Church, who do sometimes take her for granite,
    We converts tend to be more solemn, I suppose,"
Joked Miss Knight. I did not believe myself a convert,
    Nor more than an informal catechumen yet,
Prevented by my legal status as a minor
    From a step I could not guess how I should regret.

This postponement of the inevitable error
    I owe to my father's forbidding attitude,
For which in the immemorial way of children
    I felt, and expressed, at the time no gratitude.
It was thanks to his heavy-handed ultimatum
    That my first encounter with the eternal rock

Proved a close shave rather than a head-on collision;
    Not till five years later did I sustain the shock.
How, as soon as I was free to, I took the headlong
    Plunge in the baptismal font may be read about
In a privately printed "Confessional Poem"
    Written decades after the fact, called *In & Out*.
Far from an irreversible total immersion,
    It was easier coming out than going in;
What I sought from the sacraments was fire insurance
    And a deterrent to incendiary sin.
When my father, who confounded the Scarlet Woman
    Implausibly with my subfusc librarian,
Warned me against her wiles and wicked machinations,
    I laughed at him for an authoritarian,
Ironically, authoritarianism
    Being alpha and omega for Catholics,
Who, acknowledging all ten Mosaic commandments,
    Pay utmost assiduous lip-service to Six.
For every sermon, whether thundered from the pulpit
    Or muttered in the confessional, against greed
Or envy, there were dozens on the crime of Onan
    And his mysterious, misunderstood misdeed.
Never having heard of coitus interruptus—
    How could I?—I not unnaturally agreed
With the traditional, obvious explanation,
    And the wickedness of crying over spilt seed.
Miss Knight told the legend of S. Thomas Aquinas,
    That in his youth when he was tempted by a whore
He drove her from his chamber with a burning faggot
    With which he scorched the sign of the cross on the door.
On how in later life he overcompensated
    Orally for this, she did not expatiate,
Apart from the sanctimonious supposition
    That he ate in order to ratiocinate.
That the true tempter is a disembodied spirit,
    One would never suspect from listening to her.
The darkest as it were intangible transgressions
    Paled in comparison to anything 'impure.'
While the Roman Catholic emphasis on morals

87

Extolled a recurrent ritual purity,
My upbringing having stressed the Protestant ethics
Of industry, thrift, and strict veracity,
I often found the discrepancy disconcerting:
Not even Miss Knight was quite as truthful as I,
A Protestant virtue that cannot but seem priggish
To anyone whose faith is founded on a lie.

Uncertain whether to be flattered or insulted
By her references to "converts like ourselves",
I felt miscatalogued, like those out-of-place volumes
I helped Miss Knight track down on the library shelves,
Mildly bemused by the librarianly habit
Of overriding modest authorial whims
And concealing under their proper names all writers
Better known to the public by their pseudonyms.
This indicates another professional failing,
From which bibliophobia might be inferred:
The speed with which they soon converted to computers
Shows what librarians think of the printed word.
Even Miss Knight feared my curious fascination
With volumes on the upper shelves beyond my reach,
Not to mention my rather haphazard employment
Of novel turns of phrase and strange figures of speech,
Might aggravate my unorthodox inclinations.
I had so much more to learn than her Church to teach.
She twitted me with a parable illustrating
The moral pitfalls of intellectual pride,
To which she thought me, among other sins, addicted,
Proving the mind, above all, must be mortified!
It happened that not long after her own reception
Into the fold, she had gone to confession, once,
To a priest who gave her five Hail Maries as penance.
Indignant at being mistaken for a dunce,
"Really, Father," she haughtily expostulated,
"I am not an illiterate peasant." "No doubt,"
Her ghostly confessor riposted with a chuckle,
"Very well, if you prefer, you may write them out."
At the time I may have misunderstood the moral:

Surely confessional poetry, which begins
In self-examination as a kind of penance
   Inevitably ends in writing out one's sins?

Near the end of February my fourteenth birthday,
   Not so much celebrated as barely observed
In passing, brought perfunctory congratulations
   Moreover, in my opinion, hardly deserved
For the achievement of having outlived my childhood,
   Its demise demonstrated by the lack of fuss
That marked the occasion: anything like a party
   My father pronounced tasteless and superfluous.
Not only might Miss Knight never have been invited
   From motives of theological odium,
I could not have got up the nerve to ask Don Wisdom,
   Pathetically certain that he would not come.
Had I been Jewish I should have had a Bar Mitzvah,
   And as a Catholic I could have been confirmed;
Protestantism provided no rite of passage,
   Unless putting on long trousers might so be termed?
But such an assumption of the *toga virilis*
   Of late had lost its primitive significance
Now that even the little kids in kindergarten,
   Of both sexes, customarily wore long pants,
Whereas none of my pubescent contemporaries
   Would have dared to be seen dead in public in shorts,
Which when not simply a lowly masculine undergarment
   Were worn under protest for compulsory sports.
So my father toasted me in tepid cocoa,
   Tepidly wishing me Many Happy Returns,
And in grudging recognition of my ambitions
   Gave me The Poetical Works of Robert Burns.
I preferred The Poems of Gerard Manley Hopkins
   Miss Knight's gift, in part for the sake of the S.J.
After his name: an unfortunate illustration
   Of how the convert's lot was anything but gay.
I saw nothing intrinsically queer in Sprung Rhythm:
   Was not ordinary speech nothing if not sprung?
Miss Knight soon regretted her choice, having forgotten

The mimic susceptibility of the young.
Deploring my facile experimentalism,
    Natural and healthy at my unruly time
Of life, she blinked at my obscurity and shuddered
    At the liberties I took with metre and rhyme.

But it was a book called One Hundred Chinese Poems
    Which I found for myself on the library shelf
That proved the most rewarding of my birthday presents,
    The means whereby I gave myself back to myself.
While I could not measure their merit as translations—
    My own efforts in that medium still unSung—
I found these verses less bewilderingly foreign
    Than my incomprehensible ancestral tongue.
Their exoticism exercised an enchantment
    Disproportionate to their intrinsic appeal,
Influencing not only my poetic practice
    But my practical grasp of what I came to feel
Was a world and a way of life so absolutely
    Alien, remote, and indifferent to me
As to make my problems seem somehow unimportant.
    This sense of my insignificance set me free,
The view implicit in the oriental outlook
    That history is long, its latitude immense,
And my preoccupations relatively petty.
    What did the universe care for my continence?
(I little guessed that in contemporary China,
    Unlike mythical Cathay which recent events
Had swept from the face of the earth, my predilections
    Would be penalized as a capital offense.)
A forbidden pleasure becomes almost a duty
    Once you cease to resist it as a mortal sin,
But after months of undeviating resistance
    It was not without misgivings that I gave in.
Relief so long refused comes as an anticlimax;
    However I comforted myself as I curled
Up in bed with The Book of Changes "Doth it profit
    A man to save his own soul and lose the whole world?"

MARCH: ASH WEDNESDAY

Immediately the miasma of depression
    That weighed on my vital spirits began to lift,
As if my selfish denial were the expression
    Of a grief swiftly mitigated by my gift,
Not unlike the eleemosynary present
    A classmate claimed to have received for his birthday:
Nothing expensive, only a hole in his pocket
    So he would always have something with which to play.
This act, private by definition, although rarely
    Performed in public then in general denied,
I kept to myself, and when closely cross-examined
    By my prurient friend in the lunchroom I lied.
It was part of my privileged pact with the devil
    That this would be nobody's business but my own.
How could anyone take reasonable exception
    To something I did habitually alone?
Holus-bolus the anathema, *antisocial*,
    Than which society can conceive of none worse,
Is applied to the solitary noncomformist
    With the haphazard accuracy of a curse.
So any self-respecting, would-be universal
    I.e. catholic, monolithic tyranny
Has understood for millennia the importance
    Of invading and disparaging privacy.

So I continued, then, to avert my eyes in the locker
    Room, and maintained a prim silence at certain jokes
Like references to "keeping it up for hours",
    And cynical allusions to "different strokes."
Once when I was unduly dilatory dressing,
    A dripping stripling requested I dry his back.
I did so, rubbing him down with a paper towel,
    But my businesslike briskness took us both aback.
Strange that I remained superficially isolated

From those of whom I was fundamentally fond,
Whose casual, firm grasp of solitary practice
    Constituted a guilty but cohesive bond.
The wonder, at that age and in such circumstances,
    Lay not in resuming this innocuous wrong,
But in resisting an ever-present temptation
    At the flood tide of puberty, and for so long.
Six months in the annals of hasty adolescence
    Comes to seem a nearly inconceivable time,
Lost in my case, which I determined to recapture
    If only in the crude expedient of rhyme.

I who had feared the nocturnal sin of emission,
    (Committed in spite of my conscious vigilance),
After my moral, or immoral, manumission,
    Welcomed each night's conspiratorial advance.
In a line which I had stumbled across when scanning,
    At the back of the class, a French anthology,
One I cannot translate but wish that I had written,
    Tu reclamais le soir; il descend; le voici.
Evening, which in late afternoon descended,
    Offered carte blanche, cover and occasion as well.
How often I repeated coming home at nightfall,
    Voici le soir charmant, ami du criminel.
Not that I still thought, whatever the world's opinion,
    My selfish gratification to be a crime,
Rather, as most of my fellow criminals felt it,
    A clandestine albeit innocent pastime,
Unlike poor Yeats who wrote in his posthumous Memoirs,
    Which in this respect are unexpectedly frank,
Of the disgusting and debilitating habit
    For which many have the Celtic twilight to thank.
I never conceived my private practice depleted
    My creative energies, rather the reverse,
I sensed a peculiar, intimate and vital
    Connection between solitary vice and verse.
Just as poetry in a miraculous manner
    Had freed me and restored me to myself again,

So in gratitude for my new self-satisfaction
    I put away my penance and took up my pen.

Or, more appropriately, my brush: the example
    Of Chinese poetry, or what I understood
As such, proved extraordinarily seductive,
    And, like the effect of other seductions, good.
Ignorant of the original, imitative
    Of the ungrammatical structure of Chinese,
My poems became more or less ideographic,
    Written in a bastard sort of telegraphese
Deplored by Miss Knight, to whom of course I continued
    To show my work ingenuously for a while.
When the flowers of friendship faded friendship faded,
    As she found more to disapprove of than my style.
The vivid imagery I considered essential
    To a poem then was not confined to the page,
Overflowing (on account of my sloppy brushwork)
    In oils and watercolours, gouache, crayon and collage.
I learned, though I did not know it, a precious lesson,
    As the best lessons are learnt, without studying:
It is the visually oriented poet
    Who understands the poem as a plastic thing
With the free-standing, objective stature a statue
    Has as a solid, independent artefact,
And not as a transparent vessel for emotion,
    Indifferently made and usually cracked.
Those who come to verse from a discipline like music,
    Or mathematics, or no discipline at all,
Fall back on the structural luxuries of logic
    And narrative, both in their essence temporal,
And tend to become, inevitably, subjective—
    Why does time appear subjective while space does not?—
Inclined to treat the literary form in question
    As a mere vehicle for sentiment or thought,
At one extreme the highly structured lucubrations
    Of a music critic like George Bernard Shaw, say,
At the other the impenetrable confections,

Of an art critic like Theophile Gautier.
I was fortunate in that my own education
    Included a smattering of music and art
Which gave me not only a balanced preparation
    For my metier, but an ideal head start.

About this time then I became a Sunday painter,
    Writing and school taking up the work-a-day week.
Perhaps this penchant for physical recreation
    Sprang from my renewed feeling for my own physique.
My father, who was silent on intimate matters,
    Which he found at least as embarrassing as grief,
Accepted my new, apparently harmless hobby
    With a mixture of amusement and real relief,
Unlike writing, which he suspected as subversive,
    I was never sure exactly why or of what,
Unless of the tacit order it was his job to
    Promulgate: totalitarians fear free thought.
He even undertook to find me an art teacher.
    Mr. Manley inexplicably would not do,
Being plainly more interested in his models
    As aesthetic objects than in what his students drew.

Father taught in and ruled over an elementary
    School on Zulu Island, a low land bare of trees
In the Fraser delta, reminiscent of Holland
    And populated by what were then called D.P.s,
Displaced Persons, survivors of the European
    Conflagration: Poles and Czechs and Germans—few Jews—
Along with the flotsam of more outlandish nations,
    Chinese, Japanese, Pakistanis and Hindus.
It was the paternal, enthusiastic duty
    To transform these often incompatible clans
With their foreign dress and ways and polyglot beauty
    Into homogeneous New Canadians.
I was understandably snubbed by his alumni
    Who became my classmates in secondary school
As the son of the incomprehensible tyrant
    Who treated their accents and names with ridicule.

Anyone less sympathetic to the exotic
    Than my father it would be difficult to find;
Like Terence he considered nothing foreign human,
    In practice the vast majority of mankind.
Amid the many-hued and variously turbanned
    Members of this unruly miniscule U.N.
For years he manfully sustained the white man's burden
    Of turning niggers into coloured gentlemen.
Not that many of them were in the narrow sense coloured,
    Or what the colour-blind of today miscall black;
But, to a native like Fraser, Turk or Italian
    Seemed as aboriginal as an Arawak.
Therefore immigrants from Northern and Central Europe
    On account of their pallour enjoyed a slight edge
As honorary WASPS, amid innocent racists
    The invidious acronym of privilege.
But with the exception of such alien enclaves
    As this, in my childhood the true North strong and free
Was a solid, homogenous, white anglo-saxon
    Predominantly Protestant society.
Brought up among other British, and mainly Scottish
    Epigones, I do not suppose I ever knew
Intimately before I went back East to college
    So much as a single assimilated Jew.
But nowadays when I return there on a visit
    I am quizzed by the Customs of my native land
About my place of origin: "Barnaby, is it?"
    In an accent that I can hardly understand.

One day the mother of one of my father's pupils
    Came to consult him, an unusual event
In a scholastic environment where few parents
    Knew, so he used to complain, what P.T.A. meant—
Unless it was a sinister organization,
    Probably connected with the secret police,
Such as many of them had been all too familiar
    With in their lives in Yugoslavia or Greece?
Puzzled by this parent's fluent, imperfect English,
    Intimidated by her old world courtesy,

On learning that she and her husband both were artists,
    Unemployed at the moment, each with a degree
From the Cracow Academy, my father wondered
    If they would undertake the tutelage of me?
Mrs. Platov agreed, and then and there they settled
    All the details without my say-so, save the fee.
Willy-nilly I was packed off the following Sunday
    To Zulu Island, not one of my chosen strolls,
With my paintbox, in search of this artistic couple,
    About whom all I knew was that they were Poles
Apart who had found in the alluvial landscape
    Overlooked by mountains, itself level and damp,
An asylum hospitable to these survivors
    Of cultured Europe's cruel concentration camp.

They welcomed me warmly, not as a paying pupil,
    But as a long-awaited friend and honoured guest
With the lavish politeness of poor people
    And the unfailing courtesy of the oppressed.
Although their quarters were almost squalidly simple
    And themselves shabbily if not sordidly dressed,
There was homemade bread and homemade wine on the table,
    "For when," my hostess explained, "you will take a rest."
I have had further occasion since to contrast the
    Chilly civility of Canadian hosts
With the warmth and spontaneity of a Slavic
    Reception with all its interminable toasts.
A handsome, substantially prepossessing matron,
    Her fair hair beautifully braided in a crown,
Mrs. Platov introduced me to her small husband:
    "He speaks less good English than me. Please to sit down."
She apologized for the absence of her children,
    "All the time are asking, 'Can we go out to play?'
And maybe it is more better for learning English,
    I think, for playing is the Canadian way.
We did not play so much when I grew up in Poland.
    They are too young for you to play with anyway."
Like Miss Knight the Platovs treated me as an adult,

But they treated their own children in the same way,
Rarely reprimanding them in rapid-fire Polish,
    Almost diffidently, for making too much noise,
Their attitude to their naughty offspring suggesting
    That the only difference between men and boys
Is that men have bigger and more dangerous playthings,
    Not that I never noticed any children's toys
There except books and paper, pencils, paint and brushes.
    The small, untidy room was a domestic shrine
Of Central European post-impressionism
    Redolent of linseed oil, tea and turpentine.
On special occasions the tea-cups were replenished,
    As at my first visit, with dandelion wine
Which I thought just fine. The only time I had tasted
    Wine before had been during the communion rite
Which the Anglican Church celebrates in both species,
    A practice that unduly scandalized Miss Knight
In whose communion dry bread is fed to the people
    While the priest alone is permitted to get tight.
I suppose the Platovs were nominally Christian
    And to that accident probably owed their lives,
But I hardly ever heard them discuss religion:
    The only ikons in their house were their still lives.
But one time when I had got to know them much better,
    Well enough to open my adolescent heart
And ingenuously confess my inconsistent
    Religiosity, she said, "You are too smart
For superstition," and he said something in Polish
    Which his wife translated as "Your true faith is art."

Just how they really rated my artistic prospects
    They were too polite, and too politic, to say,
Although prodigal in practical criticism.
    Perhaps they thought, "If he cannot paint he can pay."
I could do neither. My parsimonious father
    Saw no reason why I should not be tutored free
By the interested benevolence of strangers
    For my future career, whatever that might be—

He dismissed as ridiculous my proclamation
    Of my solitary vocation, poetry.

Soon I discovered how disconcertingly easy
    Were the practical standards of most modern art,
Which dispensed with trivial disciplines like drawing,
    Thus placing the horse pointlessly behind the cart,
Or often doing without the horse altogether,
    Creating a horseless carriage that could not start.
At the Platovs' we did not depend upon nature
    And would have scorned to substitute a plaster cast.
Enamoured of such spontaneous self-expression
    And having cast off the manacles of the past,
What wonder I produced badly drawn compositions,
    Combinations of the incompetent and quaint,
Wrenched from the recesses of the imagination
    And negligent of the necessities of paint?
The untrammeled imagination soon grows seedy;
    There is no stimulus where there is no restraint.

On subsequent visits when I showed them the poems
    I had written in the approved modernist mode,
Despite or perhaps because of their sketchy English,
    They both pronounced them emphatically, "Very good."
Mrs. Platov in turn sadly recited something
    In her sentimental and dental native tongue
Which she declared with a sigh she herself had written,
    "When I was your age, or maybe not yet so young."
As to my verses' sometimes equivocal content,
    Either they did not notice or they did not care,
Delighted, I suspect, to see I had discovered
    A medium less uncompromising than their
Exacting one in which to express my frustration,
    For with brush and pencil I remained so unsure,
Defeated by the difficulties of the human
    Body, that ineptitude kept my pictures pure.
Nor was my poetry erotically explicit
    In those days, inhibited though my verse was free;

Ignorance and the contemporary convention
    Involved my meaning in decent obscurity.
Hence no doubt the hermeticism of my early
    Work, which occasioned so much critical remark.
For me, the world was a closed book, like my own feelings,
    Their motions mysterious and their motives dark.

The world looked dark to the Platovs, too, with more reason:
    Their profound, prolonged and painful experience
Of it had resulted in no illumination
    But in a darkness the more desperately dense
For being buried in impenetrable silence
    By their all too understandable reticence.
Yet one Sunday they shewed me, without verbal comment,
    Charcoal drawings done in a concentration camp,
Which instead of their usual chiaroscuro
    Had the merciless clarity of an arc lamp.
More than in the Doré illustrations of Dante,
    Here I recognized the lineaments of hell,
Which rather than pricking my childish carnal fancy
    Filled me with a horror and pity hard to tell
Apart. Emaciated and dejected figures
    Slumped in attitudes of unspeakable despair
Against a background of barbed wire, watch towers, chimneys,
    And all were bald and had the same subhuman stare.
Although it may seem impossible, and indecent,
    To make artistic copy of the holocaust,
Those have the privilege, and duty, of recording
    What cannot be forgotten who have paid the cost,
As I had not, in suffering; for I had never
    Witnessed anything comparable to the pain
Dissected on those tattered scraps of flimsy paper,
    And could only pray that I never would again.
This was a woe immense, perhaps unprecedented,
    That dwarfed my petty, personal unhappiness,
Although I do not share the popular opinion
    That because one's griefs are private one feels them less.
On the contrary, the many trifling discomforts

With which everyday Canadian life is crammed
Equipped me to commiserate however feebly
    The unimaginable torments of the damned.
Shewn in awful silence those shocking drawings,
    The dirtiest, I believe, I have ever seen,
I was more profoundly horrified—and embarrassed—
    Than by anything the censor might call obscene.
For this was the greatest obscenity, not only
    In our century but throughout history,
The debasement of human beings, whether guilty
    Or innocent, to some inhuman theory.
No violence enlivened this dying, no torture
    Such as renders the crucifixion picturesque,
But an utter ruin of the body and spirit,
    Grim, graceless, gratuitous, gruesome and grotesque.

Sent to the Platovs' originally to study
    Art, I came away a confirmed student of verse
And, what is not necessarily more important,
    With intimations of a cruel universe.
Once stripped of the stupid prejudice that abounded
    In my native stuffy and unenlightened milieu,
My confused sympathies uncritically confounded
    Slav, Armenian, Indian, Gypsy and Jew.
But I could not confuse the cultivated Platovs
    With the mythical objects of the ridicule
(Though the ethnic joke had not yet come into fashion)
    Retailed, I blush to say, at home as well as school.
Nevertheless I was not altogether sorry
    When the time came to quit their claustrophobic lair,
Escape their slightly cloying kindness and reenter
    The raw but reinvigorating river air.
That March through Zulu Island's rich and smelly delta
    Between flooded fields, down roads raised on narrow dikes,
Sometimes walking home I nervously in the distance
    Discerned solitary or gregarious bikes,
Among which none seemed to belong to Donald Wisdom
    Whom I dreamt of bumping into on lonely hikes.

Now bikes meant boys, and naturally I felt nervous
    Of the unpredictable plural. Friendly waves
Turned into fists clenched at a solitary paleface
    When tribal solidarity made them all braves.
Though treeless, Zulu Island had the reputation
    Of a jungle, where nothing but the jungle law
Governed the younger denizens in their brief season,
    Of whom respectable citizens went in awe.
Yet I had read the Jungle Book with fascination:
    Were not these outlaws like me about Mowgli's age?
I soon discovered that I preferred my adventures
    Set securely circumscribed by the printed page.
Selfconsciously I was wary of all encounters
    With my contemporaries unless supervised,
Aware that I must seem a solitary sissy
    To those whom I obscurely desired and despised.
Neither really bad nor dangerous but pathetic,
    They devoted their time to crimes that did not pay,
In their minor delinquency and mild defiance
    Obeying the poet's advice to seize the day,
Which they did with a vengeance, guessing that tomorrow,
    Condemned to drudgery less lucrative than crime,
They must forego the late delights of Daylight Saving
    And live out the rest of their lives on Standard Time.
Perhaps they envied me my comparative freedom
    In a future it would be futile to avenge?
That I was my father's son did not make things better;
    I became an innocent object of revenge.
It was hard to believe, when I was in their power,
    That in the years to come our roles would be reversed,
And that the era of my independence elsewhere
    Would see their collective despotism dispersed.
The elements were individually harmless,
    Amiable sometimes and seldom impolite,
But these agreeable atoms became a menace
    When mutual attraction moved them to unite.
Most times they passed me by in minatory silence
    On neutral territory such as in the halls

At school, their passage punctuated in the open
  By ambiguous whistles, laughter, and cat-calls.

Once when I was coming from art class they surprised me
  On Zulu Island where there was no place to hide.
Although I could see their bicycles in the offing,
  I would not run away, vainly detained by pride,
Or greeting as inevitable this encounter—
  Besides, I could not run as fast as they could ride.
Soon enough they surrounded me, some half-a-dozen
  Youths my senior, as well as my superiors
In strength and a certain sort of sophistication,
  Impatient to settle imaginary scores.
"Whaddya got there?" I handed over my sketchbook
  (Without much expectation of getting it back)
To him I had identified as the leader,
  Assuming there must be one in every pack,
A boy of arresting Nordic, no, Arctic beauty,
  With icy eyes and hair so blonde that it looked white,
(Which makes him sound too like a sinister albino,
  Which, despite his extreme pallour, he was not quite),
Balanced astride his bicycle among his cohorts,
  Apparently poised for either attack or flight.
"What do you want?" I asked. Amid sarcastic laughter
  The young ring-leader superciliously smiled.
I recognized the Nazi gangster in the Viking
  And the unpredictable bully in the child.
Riffling quickly through the smudged and disfigured pages
  My precocious critic, who had a German name,
Paused at the portrait of a mysterious woman,
  Draped. "What's the matter? Can't you draw a naked dame?"
The others crowding to ogle over his shoulder
  In their disappointment found plenty to deride
In my drawing, some making indecent suggestions
  Regarding the probable upshot had I tried.
The first time I confronted sexual fascism,
  Tongue-tied I was saved by not knowing what to say.
My tormentors assumed I shared their predilections,
  And I could not have disabused them anyway.

Hitler's victims who wore the lavendar triangle
    Are dishonoured by silence even to this day.

Oppressed by a sneaking sense of a certain weakness
    For my captors which complicated my distress,
I masked with a facade of contemptuous silence
    Sentiments it would be fatal for them to guess.
Allegations of complicity in the victim,
    Which are oftener than not monstrously unjust,
Gain a faint plausibility when the oppressor
    Is the surreptitious object of guilty lust.
Not only willing participants in those brutal
    But harmless exercises known as S & M,
But anyone attacked by adolescent bullies
    Entertains latent ambivalence towards them.
Ironically the hooligans who inspected
    My blameless notebooks hopefully for something raw
Might have provided the imaginary models
    I was too inhibited and inept to draw.
Their very arrogant, animalistic poses
    Had all the unconscious grace of a Grecian frieze,
So that, as they bestrode their metal steeds, I envied
    The unfeeling machinery between their knees.
Their straightforward prurience presently grew weary
    Of my water-colours, preferring other sport,
And, after playing half-hearted catch with my sketchbook,
    Off they rode triumphant: their triumph would be short.
In half a mile I retrieved my discarded art work
    But could not so quickly retrieve myself. Escaped
Physically unhurt, merely humiliated,
    I had the queer sensation of having been raped
Gregariously, without putting up a struggle.
    I made my way home in a post-traumatic trance,
Bedevilled by regret and resentment, as shaken
    And naked as if they had taken off my pants.

Imagine my discomfiture a few weeks later
    Meeting one of the gang at an informal dance.
I had been invited to a small birthday party

By a girl I had known ever since the first grade;
Although far from Hallowe'en, like all teenage socials
    It was something of a selfconscious masquerade,
Exactly the same kind of stuffy get-together
    As those I remember from my earliest years,
Such as the nursery tea I had once disrupted
    Attempting to get the attention of my peers,
As rocking on a hobbyhorse I babbled
    Of the primal scene witnessed in a field of flax
Where an older boy and his girl had demonstrated
    To my astonished delight the beast with two backs.
But the other four-year-olds were not interested,
    My revelations fell on indifferent ears
As if I preached to the incomprehending heathen.
    Frustrated and unheeded, I burst into tears.
Present company, although presumably better
    Informed, appeared at first glance improbably prim.
Our hostess did her best to dispell this impression
    With low music and lights irreligiously dim.
Too old for games (we thought), and too shy for flirtation,
    Too dumb for conversation, and too young to drink,
We sat about like strangers in a railway station—
    As easily break the ice in a skating rink!
The greedy gravitated to a groaning sideboard
    Laden with the makings of a rather late lunch:
Hot dogs, cold slaw, potato chips, potato salad
    As well as a tasteless kind of Temperance Punch.
The background music, anodyne and sentimental,
    On the eve of the eruption of rock and roll,
Was diversified by an old, upright piano
    Pounding out hits like "In the Mood", and "Heart and Soul",
To which some of the more brazen girls began dancing
    With one another, selfconsciously, two by two,
While their intended partners gazed on from the sidelines,
    Uneasily aware they should be dancing too.
In similar but more coercive circumstances
    At school the sexes tended to stay separate,
Most boys looking on the young female of their species
    As the male praying mantis might look on his mate.

* * *

But what was he doing here with these well-dressed children?
    Clad in turtleneck sweater and corduroy pants,
The roughneck whom I recognized from Zulu Island,
    Stepped up and without preamble asked me to dance.
Astounded, I accepted. It seemed not to matter
    That I did not really know how: neither did he,
So our exaggeratedly clumsy performance
    Was applauded as a plausible parody.
Till I realized with a thrill of recognition
    The point of this hitherto footling exercise:
If dancing with girls had always felt like a duty,
    Dancing with my own sex was a pleasant surprise.
Being older, more masculine-looking and bigger,
    My impetuous partner masterfully led,
While servile but inefficient I tried to follow,
    Two beats behind the music or two steps ahead.
Galvanized by our unconventional example,
    The embarrassed waxworks began to move about.
Soon the living-room was filled with gyrating couples.
    My vis-a-vis whispered, "Want to sit this one out?"
Our inauspicious first encounter unforgotten
    But unmentioned, we shyly confided first names—
His was Dick—and biographical information.
    To this day I do not quite understand his aims.
He had come honestly by his fisherman's jersey
    Working weekends on the family fishing boat,
An old trawler which he offered to show me over
    And described as "the leakiest bugger afloat."
His language, like his looks and his dress and his manners,
    Vigorous, virile, and disconcertingly coarse,
However out of place in such polite surroundings,
    Had a crude but undeniably telling force.
At the same time he was unexpectedly gentle
    As he threw his arms about my shoulders and pressed
Me unprepared, not unflattered but flabbergasted,
    Feebly protesting against his broad, woolly chest.
"Pretend," he whispered in my tingling ear, "We're necking,"
    (A decade later he might have said, "making out".)

A joke conceived in the same satyrical spirit
    As his first invitation to the dance, no doubt.
As he embraced me with exaggerated ardour
    I exaggerated my struggles to resist,
But amid the nervous, apotropaic laughter
    Felt for the first time what it was to be kissed,
Even facetiously in public, by a stranger,
    Squarely or rather orotundly on the lips,
Mortified by my rapidity of reaction
    To many of the tongue's inarticulate slips;
No less puzzled in retrospect by the reception
    Of our misconduct by innocent girls and boys
Who saluted our embrace with vocal amusement,
    So naughtiness was made innocuous by noise.
It seemed that one could get away almost with murder
    If the crime were committed *coram publico*,
For we were regarded not so much as performing
    An unnatural act as putting on a show,
In ostensible and ostentatious derision
    Of the mores of more conventional romance.
This time our audience, abjuring imitation,
    Continued childishly to chat and snack and dance.
Discovering the dilemma of the performer
    Who overidentifies with his or her part,
My performance, which owed everything to nature,
    I tried to attribute, transparently, to art.
I had never experienced, nor yet imagined,
    Such, in the phrase from *Fidelio,* nameless joy.
The absurd antics, on the screen, of men and women,
    Acquiring undreamt-of dimensions with a boy—
Not exactly undreamt-of: had I not awakened
    Often from the vague impression of an embrace
With the object of my long-standing admiration
    Whom fantasy inserted in a stranger's place,
And whose absence, inexplicable as the presence
    At a private party of this likeable lout,
Prevented me perhaps from putting into practice
    Perversities I now was finding out about?
The idea of doing such things with Don Wisdom

Intensified my hypothetical disgust
At squandering on an indifferent acquaintance
    The treasures of love found in the junk shop of lust.
In addition to the venereal excitement
    Mere proximity was sufficient to provoke,
Suffused by a novel sensation of connivance
    As a participant in the amorous joke
Which like all such jokes became less and less amusing
    With every delicious moment it was prolonged,
I reluctantly forsook our ludicrous posture
    And the arms in which I made believe I belonged.
The whole business lasted no more than a few minutes.
    We stopped our fooling as soon as the laughter died.
The episode seemed immediately forgotten
    But for my agitation, which was hard to hide.
For the rest of the evening we kept our distance
    Till it was time to go, when gruffly he proposed
Seeing me home: although in different directions,
    Our routes lay closer together than I supposed.
Soon, as if to short-circuit our mutual shyness,
    He unexpectedly reached out and grabbed my hand,
Scratching my palm—this was "the electrician's handshake"
    Which, while shocked, I pretended not to understand.

At his insistence we took the sinister short-cut
    Through the ill-illumined labyrinth of the park,
Which I had been expressly forbidden to enter,
    For mysterious reasons, ever after dark.
As an omnivorous reader, I had devoured the
    Gothic extravagances of popular lore:
The overly familiar face outside the window—
    Where have you seen it, or something like it, before?
Insinuating fingers fumbling for admittance,
    Too insistent and sympathetic to ignore?
These bloodthirsty noctambulists' contagious passion
    Suggests another equivocal metaphor.
As victims multiply as rapidly as crosses
    Each inevitably becomes a predator.
The scenario owed to hoary superstition

Less than to Victorian prejudice and art.
A rival in love, once, of Oscar Wilde, Bram Stoker
    Described Dracula as a dandified up-start.
The undead, the unconventional, the unmarried
    In respectable society have no part;
And those who retire at sunrise obscenely sated
    With every encounter risk a stake through the heart.

Holding hands, as innocuous and comforting as
    Holding someone or being held in someone's arms,
Gave me perhaps unrealistic reassurance
    Of protection from all supernatural harms.
That my protector was himself perfectly harmless
    In spite of or because of his frightening size,
His uncouth yet diffident and courteous courtship
    Led me at once hopeful and helpless to surmise.
Whistling in the dark, a figurative expression
    For a cheerful pretense that effectively cheers,
Might have heartened me, except that I could not whistle
    Any more than I could have quite defined my fears.
At that age the slightest difference in our ages
    Gapped larger than it was ever to do again:
From the perspective of fourteen, overgrown children
    Of fifteen and sixteen already looked like men.
Though only chronologically my senior
    By a year or two, he seemed of another sphere,
Like an inhabitant of an alien planet—
    But what, I kept wondering, was he doing here?
He saw me home unenlightened and unmolested,
    Whatever that means: it is one transitive verb
That loses a lot of its menace in translation:
    In Spanish, No Molestar means, Do Not Disturb.
Bidding me goodnight at the door to my apartment
    He asked if he could see me again the next day.
The prospect of tomorrow filled me with misgiving,
    But I nodded my acquiescence anyway.
"O.K." he mumbled, "I'll pick you up at eleven
    And show you over my old man's effing boat."
I figured that F stood for fishing, but could not fathom

The implications of his promissory note.
I went to bed in a fog of diffuse excitement
    Which took solidity in an erotic dream,
A naked masquerade of stationary leap-frog
    And similar variations of the same theme.

The next morning, however, I was dressed and ready
    For this mystery excursion long before nine.
My father, whom I had told of the invitation,
    To my astonishment forbade me to decline:
"Go ahead. Do you good to get out a little.
    Teach you a thing or two to see over this ship."
Encouraging me to embark on fresh friendship,
    "Maybe he'll ask you along on a fishing trip."
How could my father, with his upright and old-fashioned,
    Even narrow-minded notions of discipline,
Urge a seemingly innocuous course of action
    That might result in what he must regard as sin?
Of course I had not told him the unexpurgated
    Story—what normal boy in my position would?
Nor could, nor can, I understand my hesitation,
    For what did I stand to gain as a goody-good?

While waiting I set up my easel in the bedroom,
    The only spot where I could hope to be alone.
In our crowded, compulsively tidy apartment
    There was no little corner I could call my own.
Presently my father went out to do the shopping
    Leaving me alone, which was quite all right with me;
Only those who have lived for some time in close quarters
    Know the precarious pleasure of privacy.
I was working on a murky, ambitious canvas
    Symbolic of something, but what I did not know,
Which combined the technical skill of Grandma Moses
    With the flamboyant fantasy of Gustave Moreau.
For once hereabouts a splendidly sunny morning
    Infiltrated the unlovely Venetian blinds
As I daubed away at my dismal composition,
    Distinctly—maybe indistinctly—of two minds.

What apprehension caused my ambivalent fidgets?
    From what did I hope for a last-minute reprieve?
For all my recent, and relative, liberation,
    I remained nonetheless relatively naive,
Ignorant of the names, let alone the descriptions,
    Of the overtures I was apprehensive of,
The advances I had retreated from already,
    Much more so the mechanics of making love.
How could anyone make that which is uncreated,
    Engendered by an exceptional act of grace?
Perversely again I prayed for the unexpected
    To arrive in my expected visitor's place,
Though I suspect my transcendental love of Wisdom
    Merely meant I admired the beauty of his face,
Which was taking shape, independent of volition
    Or effort on the canvas now before my eyes,
The first likeness I had achieved, an apparition
    And, like most apparitions, a complete surprise.
When interrupted by the irrelevant doorbell
    I found I had forgotten all about my date:
There is nothing like an absorbing occupation
    While one is waiting to make one forget to wait.
But Dick was leaning impatiently on the buzzer
    With an exuberance I hated to deflate.
As I opened the door he seemed to fill the doorway
    With his expansive presence and expanded chest,
Looking rather less prepossessing than last evening,
    Though as far as I could tell identically dressed.
He demanded with a broad leer if I were ready,
    Though it must have been obvious that I was not;
I lied: I had forgotten, besides, I was busy . . .
    He followed me inside uninvited. "With what?"
Recognizing his rival in the picture
    By its inadvertent verisimilitude,
He remarked, "Not bad, but you need a better model.
    How would you like me to pose for you—in the nude?"
It was, in retrospect, a kind of ultimatum,
    But prudence and prudery together forbade
Taking any notice of his immodest offer,

So to my covert regret he stayed fully clad.
Again, not for the last time, I found myself playing
    The thankless part of the unhappy hypocrite,
And when I postponed our nautical expedition
    Sine die, Dick commented succinctly, "Shit!"
Dishonestly I pled parental disapproval,
    Which he (though God the Father has no Christian name)
On learning my surname acquiesced in, believing
    His principal and not my principles to blame.
That I should repent of this desperate, defensive
    Deception in the emptiness of time much less
Than of my perverse and obstinate refusal
    I could not then know, or did I already guess?
Such a lie must bring immediate retribution,
    Whether or not I realized it at the time.
With a shrug Dick took his disappointed departure,
    So the punishment coincided with the crime.
He stalked out of my life for good or ill forever,
    As unpredictably as he had stumbled in,
If not quite naked with stocking feet in my chamber
    In the words of Wyatt, yet behovely as sin.

When he returned Fraser was furious to find me
    Still painting, and upbraided me at unfair length
For my lack of enterprise. In extenuation,
    I might have pled mortal frailty or moral strength,
Uncomfortably aware that I had been tempted
    Once again and, because unscathed by Cupid's skill,
Had again escaped. With chagrin I contemplated
    The trumpery, temporary triumph of will.
Had I not in my short-sighted thoughtlessness chosen
    Over the nonsense of life the essence of art?
As if a daubed canvas were any consolation
    For an unbroken hymen or a broken heart!
So, I was moved by that moving picture, The Heiress,
    And its prosy predecessor, Washington Square
Whose celibate, verbose, and expatriate author
    Had made the same choice, unhappily unaware
Of all of the future miracles of revision

That would be inspired by this present despair.
From time to time and always at a certain distance
    I saw Dick again, often as not with his gang
On their bicycles, and we passed without a greeting
    But never, on my part at least, without a pang.

APRIL FOOLS' DAY

On first looking into Aristotle's *Poetics*
    Most readers, surprised by the emphasis on plot
As opposed to character, wonder why the action
    Should matter more than the actors: not who but what?
This seems to reverse the perceived natural order
    Where the player rather than the play is the thing,
As we were taught in English class when reading Hamlet,
    How to 'analyze the character of the king'.
Such widespread academic misinterpretation
    One may also characteristically see
In practice in certain popular entertainments
    Like serials and situation comedy.
There character may be seen to dictate the action,
    Even the universal traits of everyman
Predicating each new predictable dénouement
    Rather than some grand, over-all dramatic plan.
The reason behind this inveterate inversion
    Of the Aristotelean priorities
Seems to be that our myopic human condition
    Cannot see the existential woods for the trees.
So rich in incident as to seem incoherent,
    Life lacks all apparent pattern, save the abstract
Imposed by retrospect, which can never be final,
    Since nobody alive has sat through the last act.
Other lives may present the illusion of meaning
    In epitome; one's own remains meaningless
From moment to moment, though psychoanalytic
    Theory pretends to make some sense of the mess.
In the midst of the action baffled by the action,
    The one objective fact to which everyone clings
Is the palpable solidity of the other
    Participants, puppets on invisible strings.
While in everyday life the dramatis personae
    Appear all too obvious, the drama does not;

To an actor surrounded by actors, no wonder
    The play has plenty of characters but no plot.

All of this pretentious, preposterous preamble
    Serves to introduce a new character on stage,
An entrance usually following an exit
    As naturally as turning over a page
In life as often as in art, in adolescence
    Especially, that impatient, page-turning age.
At the library the reign of Miss Knight was waning
    Under the dawning influence of Mr. Day
(Which is the way to pronounce his symbolic surname,
    Though being Icelandic, he spelled it D A J),
Who, enlightening me concerning my condition,
    Always insisted that he himself was not gay,
A frivolous-sounding American expression
    I cannot imagine him using anyway.
After supper one humid evening in April
    I slipped off to the library, which closed at 9,
With The Tale of Genji by Lady Murasaki
    Almost overdue, anxious to avoid a fine.
I found to my surprise that the presiding presence
    Behind the circulating desk was not Miss Knight
Or one of her formidable feminine colleagues
    Who might have originated the term 'up-tight',
But an easy-going if quizzical male stranger
    Who nonetheless seemed to recognize me on sight.
In those days masculine librarians were something
    That the ordinary borrower seldom saw;
I regarded this unmanly manifestation
    With a curiosity uncoloured by awe.
That certain ancient and honourable professions
    Should traditionally attract the homophile
Seems undeniable: dress-design, ballet dancing,
    Any metier that requires a sense of style,
Like interior decoration and hair-dressing,
    Draws some men in a manner of speaking like flies.
Although every occupation has its quota,

A queer construction worker comes as a surprise,
Whereas most art historians and harpsichordists,
    High episcopalian priests and organists
Are notoriously limp-wristed: I wonder
    Sometimes if a straight male librarian exists—
An anomaly I ought sooner to have welcomed,
    Had I known it, with gratitude than with alarm
For Mr. Daj's unacknowledged orientation
    Did me in the long run the opposite of harm.

Informal acquaintance flowered into friendship
    Slowly, by adolescent standards—in a week;
Often the only patron when Daj was on duty,
    I found it only common courtesy to speak.
The time I returned *The Tale of Genji* unfinished,
    Although we had not been properly introduced,
He engaged me in literary conversation
    Calculated to give my vanity a boost,
Suggesting that since I seemed to like long novels
    I should try the novel *longueurs* of Marcel Proust,
Which he recommended in Scott-Moncrieff's translation,
    Itself, he hastened to proclaim, a masterpiece.
But if length were the chief criterion of merit,
    I wonder why he did not lend me *War and Peace*?
And are there not novels equally long in English?
    The motives for his choice became all too plain,
When he told me to omit the earlier volumes
    And start straightaway with *The Cities of the Plain.*
At once appalled by the author's tortured, translated
    Style, I was agog at what he was tortured by,
Which seemed to derive from a real-life bent for torture
    And a warped disinclination for saying I.
Yet despite his ostensible disapprobation,
    There is something unmistakably partisan
In the prurient pages Proust devotes to Sodom;
    The unnatural attraction of man to man
He diagnosed a disease, an involuntary
    Disability which is probably innate:

No accident the paederast Charlus should also
    The hereditary principle incarnate.

Beginning the book as instructed in the middle
    Much like an archaeologist sinking a trench
In a mound, I discovered a different city
    When I reread it from the beginning in French.
But while *Remembrance of Things Past* became my bible
    For a time, a text inspired and in that sense true,
I was never to feel the same enthusiasm,
    However, for *A la Recherche du Temps Perdu.*
Sacred scripture presupposes a sacred language,
    Normally that to which one is exposed when young.
Once at the Wailing Wall I heard two British tourists
    Marvel at hearing the Jews, "in their native tongue"
Recite the psalms—the language in which they were written
    Originally, or antiphonally sung.
Such insular naivete seems universal,
    The Ursprache only the dialect one knows.
Too often the poetry of youth, in translation,
    Turns out to have been at best indifferent prose.

And what of the librarian who introduced me
    To the subtle, seductive universe of Proust?
I should state at the outset that he never seduced me,
    Perhaps sensing my reluctance to be seduced.
Prudery apart, which was rapidly eroding
    In principle if not yet in physical fact,
At that age I just did not think adults attractive
    Nor even capable of the physical act;
That there were grown men of a similar persuasion
    I must have known but did not personally care,
Untroubled by their imaginary attentions
    And of my own immature charms quite unaware.
What is called in France le detournement des mineurs
    Is surely a misnomer: obviously they
Are not deflected from their proper or improper
    Course, but encouraged prematurely in the way.
In my case of course the only means of corruption

Was mental or psychological—on the whole
The most insidious and effectual method,
    Granted that the soul alone can corrupt the soul.
At this moment legislation is being mooted
    Which would have stunted my development if passed,
Making librarians responsible for certain
    Books they lend—such as the *Remembrance of Things Past?*
Like most libraries ours maintained a locked collection,
    Certain vintages vintners reserved for themselves,
Lady Chatterley, Ulysses, Tropic of Cancer,
    Harmless compared to some stuff on the open shelves.
Thus my carnal curiosity was excited
    By one sentence in a forgotten mystery
Describing how a boy in a Portugese brothel
    Wore a blue ribbon to mark his virginity;
Mine was intact but decently undecorated;
    What puzzled me was the significance of blue.
A dangerous book may be any work of fiction
    Which the ingenuous reader supposes true,
The most pernicious being the books of the Bible,
    The source of much historical hullaballoo.
But that Daj was a far from ingenuous reader
    Of character, it was not difficult to see;
He had travelled far—at least as far as Toronto
    In his pursuit of a professional degree—
And might claim to have known many men's minds and cities,
    As it says in the third line of *The Odyssey.*
He must by then I suppose have been about thirty
    Years of age, and although himself a native-born
Canadian, came of undiluted Icelandic
    Stock, his Christian, or pre-Christian name being Bjorn.
Hardly handsome, he struck me first as downright homely,
    With the kind of face sometimes described as rough-hewn,
Which it never occurred to me to find forbidding,
    Any more than a pock-marked, amiable prune.
Nor did he seem smitten by my juvenile beauty—
    For most fourteen-year-olds are beautiful but blind
To their own generic, fleeting bloom. Daj was after,
    Rather, the masculine maidenhead of my mind,

Already compromised, which he planned to deflower
    By the age-old expedient of being kind.

Whenever I returned one of the works of fiction
    He had given me, with a significant look
He asked me how I'd liked it; whatever my verdict,
    He gave me another subversive bedside book.
In the course of our accelerating acquaintance
    I progressed—if it be progress—from Proust to Gide.
Where Sodom and Gomorrah had failed to corrupt me,
    Was The Immoralist more likely to succeed?

While Daj was enlightening me during the night shift,
    In the afternoon I began slighting Miss Knight,
Whom he unfairly, as a free-thinking Sarastro,
    Sniffed at as an obscurantist Queen of the Night
Who supplied me, or plied me, with Catholic writings
    Of varied worth, from Bernanos to "Bernadette",
Which he assured me with infuriating foresight
    I should before I knew it utterly forget.
Thus there arose a literary competition
    For the attention of a bookworm of fourteen.
But was there really ever a serious question
    As to which way the wavering reader would lean?
Although my faith had rapidly evaporated
    It had left behind a repulsive residue
Of scruple and superstition and inhibition
    Which would presently vanish 'like the morning dew
From the garlic leaf', in one of those Chinese poems
    That had been my undoing. If I was undone,
As Knight supposed, Daj merely completed the process
    An imaginary orient had begun;
So in the empty, brightly-lit library nightly
    We covered nearly everything under the sun.
Eventually, inevitably I showed him
    My manuscript verses, which he with eyebrow raised,
First pretended to be unable to decipher
    Then criticized and only implicitly praised.

Nothing could excite more than polite admiration
    In the printed poems he proffered in return,
With their predictable rhymes and four-footed quatrains
    And strophes that as often as not botched the turn.
When being not only callow but opinionated,
    And tactless, I allowed I thought these pretty bad,
He said he had no pretensions to be a poet,
    Though with the brashness of youth I plainly had;
But he claimed that to write, even badly, at thirty
    Was an accomplishment: who doesn't as a lad?
On the contrary, how few middle-aged beginners
    With a command of stress have I ever seen?
While the one student I have with a grasp of accent
    Seemed to have acquired it already at sixteen.
Still the child who figuratively lisped in numbers
    By a miracle somehow managed to survive
That speech impediment and, digitally fluent,
    Is counting syllables today at forty-five.
But at the time the unlikely thought of attaining
    Such a mythical age never entered my head
And formed no feature of my poetic ambition;
    By forty I guess I expected to be dead,
Like so many of my romantic predecessors,
    Keats and Shelley and Wilfred Owen and Hart Crane,
Overlooking the vast plurality of others
    Long-lived enough to know that they have lived in vain.
My direst nightmare was of outliving my talent,
    So the fashionable example of Rimbaud
Appalled me, such silence seeming much worse than Wordsworth's
    Garrulous and protracted lyric afterglow.
Life without letters struck me as empty and idle;
    What to do when I could not write I did not know.
Of that for the present at least there was no question.
    I scribbled more in those years than any time since,
Most of it fortunately lost and long forgotten,
    Otherwise I suppose I should read it and wince.
The fugitive quality that we praise as promise
    Contains much that we prize as positively bad.

April

Premature perfection proves so frequently sterile,
    Carelessness and poor taste should make talent scouts glad.

Bjorn Daj I had to admit was a timid critic
    Whose grand enthusiasm for The Shropshire Lad
As well as the polyglot rhapsodies of Whitman
    Exhibited a gay indifference to style.
His habitual, hypocritical discretion
    Concealed a combination of guilt and guile.
As reluctant as any omniscient author
    To employ plainly the first person singular,
He was fearlessly frank in his use of the second,
    'I am' being more compromising than 'You are'.
In this he reminds me of those contemporary
    Poets to whom first person pronouns seem taboo,
As in the phrase, 'You are the subject of this poem,'
    Where passim one ought to substitute I for you,
Neither you nor I possessing much definition,
    As true protagonists and antagonists do.
Thus Bjorn Daj was prepared to make a diagnosis
    In my case which he would not hazard for himself;
At the same time to facilitate my self-knowledge
    He provided access to the forbidden shelf.
"I think," he said, and pulled his cheek, a mannerism
    Of his indicative of thoughtfulness, I guess,
As idiosyncratic as his rapid, nervous,
    Automatic reiteration, "Yes, yes, yes . . ."
"I think, on the basis of your reading—and writing—
    That you will probably be homosexual."
"Really?" I marvelled to hear my intimate fumblings
    Described in so misbegotten and clinical
A term. To this day I am always disconcerted
    By definitions of my sexuality
As a perversion or sickness or social problem,
    And object to such pathology, "But that's me!"

This was precisely my reticent mentor's message,
    Received as if I suspected it all along.

It is hard to regard as heretical any
 Category to which one happens to belong;
Besides, in my bottomless innocence I doubted
 Anything that felt so natural could be wrong.
Why then is it often called 'the crime against nature'?
 Interpreting nature in the narrowest sense
As *natura naturans*, i.e. procreation,
 In the face of all the physical evidence.
Fortunately neither the Universal Doctor
 Nor some homophobic contemporary quack
Was my designated source of misinformation,
 But a late Victorian literary hack
Whose *Psychology of Sex* Bjorn Daj liberated
 From the locked bookcase where it had long lain unread.
At first puzzled by the term Sexual Inversion—
 Was one supposed to do it standing on one's head?—
I was presently not unpleasantly enlightened
 By this entertaining educational tome
Which I read in the basement when Daj was on duty,
 As it might have been disastrous to take it home,
In view of my father's emphatic disapproval
 Whenever he was reminded how young I was
By my reading habits: had he not banned *Ulysses*
 And confiscated *Rebel Without A Cause*?
Not that he would have heard of Havelock Ellis
 (Though I may underestimate the book's ill fame),
But a glance at those case histories where initials
 Illustrated the love that dared not speak its name
Must rouse his nebulous but well-founded suspicions,
 Whereupon my benefactor would be to blame.
Ironically Fraser thought Daj a splendid fellow
 When they met, in contrast to tenebrous Miss Knight,
A healthy, desirable influence, moreover,
 And for once, if for the wrong reasons, he was right,
When without conscious irony appreciating
 That Bjorn Daj is what is called in Proust 'a man's man',
A term that in ordinary parlance suggested
 Someone unquestionably virile, like Tarzan;

And so he was, who taught me the law of the jungle
    By means of a most extraordinary book,
(Today I am not sure I understand his motives,
    But I do not underestimate the risk he took.)
Which was more remarkable for having been written
    Not by a confessed member of the brotherhood
But by that rarest of rare species, an outsider
    Who not only did not condemn but understood.
Most admirable in Ellis' pioneer study
    Was its humane and humanistic tolerance,
Unlike the bias of those scientific experts
    Who adopt an impartial, that is hostile stance.
With no more than two kinds of treatment of the subject—
    Rabidly *con* and apologetically *pro*—
Not even statistics could be counted objective,
    Though Kinsey's seem to some objectionably so.
While proponents are disproportionately prudent,
    Apologizing for what they would like to hide,
Even most (rare in those days) boy meets boy romances
    Normally ending with the hero's suicide,
Cons like the pathological Doctor Kraft-Ebing,
    A prototype of the mad German scientist,
Can assert nonsense without fear of contradiction—
    An authority I found easy to resist.
But not so the irresistible Havelock Ellis,
    Whose theories I was inclined to overlook
Incurious about the cause of my condition
    But bemused by all the curious turns it took.
The stories that were the Studies' salient feature,
    And the reason it was originally banned
Except for consultation by puzzled physicians,
    Contained not a few words I did not understand
And sent me often to the Oxford Dictionary
    In vain: silent on the subject of *irrumates*,
(My schoolboy Latin did not extend to Catullus),
    Murray could hardly bring himself to define *nates*—
Which I found that I was familiar with already
    As defined in denims, chinos, corduroys,

For I followed the wide-spread custom of assessing
    The fundamental assets of assorted boys.

To describe these case histories as stimulating
    Were an understatement; that magistrate was right
Who ruled that under the protective guise of science
    Ellis pandered to a prurient appetite.
Written by various eminent men of letters
    Anonymously, the Studies' mandarin prose
Style owed a lot to the Victorian tradition
    Of left-handed literature under the rose.
I received in the spirit in which they were given
    The outpourings of so many sinister hands,
The singularities of long-dead men of standing
    And anally-oriented analysands,
With the means to hand but without the circumstances
    To satisfy the transient natural urge
Provoked by the book—besides, I believed catharsis
    Involved an exclusively emotional purge.
And this, by the time I had finished the first volume
    Of Havelock Ellis, I improbably achieved;
Like Miss Knight when she closed her Roman catechism,
    Because it appeared impossible I believed.
The impossible I had already encountered
    Second-hand, in smutty inscriptions and loose talk
In locker rooms, tales incredulously discounted
    As scatological pipe dreams or poppycock,
Couched normally in bad language, less pussy-footing,
    Sesquipedalian, learned and Latinate
Than that which I found paradoxically suggestive.
    There seemed something depraved about *manustuprate*
(The meaning of which I was forced to put together)
    That its vulgar synonym somehow seemed to lack.
Perhaps I should have been happier had I happened
    To guess that *iacio* could be the root of 'jack'?

Whatever their authors or editor intended
    These stale confessions had a similar effect

To that excited by those ancient Chinese poems
    Yet one that was inexplicably less direct
In the sense of suggesting immediate action,
    Something pornography seldom if ever does,
Providing instead its own kind of satisfaction.
    Not that I had a clue what pornography was!
Namely that it most neatly fulfills Aristotle's
    Primary prescription for all literature,
In so far as the effect it has on the reader,
    Is immediate, unmistakable, and pure.
Detective novels, science fiction, horror stories—
    Genres that serious critics tend to dismiss—
Satisfy the basic precepts of the Poetics
    Better than an ambitious farrago like this
With its casual structure and frequent digressions
    Unified by nothing but the narrative voice.
The well-made work had become an anachronism
    After the examples of Eliot and Joyce.
Nevertheless, although an uncritical modern
    Like most of the young, instinctively avant-garde,
I was in spite of my prejudices diverted
    By the odd deviant and defiant die-hard.
For what could be more old-fashioned, not to say almost
    Antediluvian, than the imputed fault
That brought divine anger down upon guilty Sodom
    And turned an innocent bystander into salt?
I emerged from my immersion in this miasma
    Morally polluted but mentally refreshed,
With the growing and uncomfortable conviction
    That the profane word had presently to be fleshed.
Flesh, or a pretty reasonable simulacrum,
    Bjorn Daj, who believed in doing such things by halves,
Provided as well as verbal specifications
    In the form of some funny physique photographs
That he had taken and developed in his darkroom
    In the course of what he called exhaustive research
Into The Mechanism of Male Detumescence—
    Science being something suspicion could not smirch.
This data was a far cry from the Book of Knowledge's

Reproductions of Roman copies of the Greeks,
Even farther from the National Geographic's
    Explorations of aboriginal physiques.
To begin with, one seldom saw the subjects' faces
    Whereas other parts less customarily seen
Were displayed in a manner frankly ostentatious
    Which some would have called not clinical but obscene.
These private parts can be surprisingly expressive
    (And, unlike the visage, do not visibly age),
But their range of expression is rather restricted—
    Lust and indifference, but neither mirth nor rage.
In our society when sizing up a stranger
    The face is the first thing at which most people stare;
Decapitated by the camera, their ages
    Hinted by the distribution of body hair,
These models had achieved the ideal, unself-conscious
    Anonymity of the absolutely bare.
Distressed to find the genitals so unaesthetic
    In themselves, for all their functional interest,
I was fascinated more by a full-length portrait
    Of a beautiful blond youth minimally dressed,
Whom I found, for he reminded me of Don Wisdom,
    Strikingly sexier than the immodest rest.
What theologians have miscalled the curse of Adam,
    For which carnal curiosity was to blame,
And the foundation garment of civilization,
    The occasion of the first fashion show was shame.
Prelapsarian sects like the Doukhobors plainly
    Display their innocence by taking off their clothes.
But those who deprecate the facts of life as filthy
    Must clean up nature's act with the vacuum she loathes.

Once Bjorn Daj had laid his cards on our kitchen table,
    Far too prudent to do so at the library,
In the shape of these stark anatomical studies,
    After closing one night, over a cup of tea,
The only oral stimulant which he permitted
    Himself. But stronger, ocular stimulants lay
On the oilcloth, where my unpredictable father,

Returned early from chairing the school P.T.A.,
Could see the damning evidence spread out before us
      Like one of those facetiously indecent decks
Designed uniquely for solitaire and strip poker
      Which combined the attractions of gambling and sex.
No wonder my old Presbyterian grandmother
      Used to call playing cards "the devil's picture book"!
That this pack was composed of jacks (or knaves) and jokers
      My father seemed more than anxious to overlook
As Bjorn Daj without haste, which might have appeared guilty,
      Shuffled the snapshots back into their envelope,
Rising to acknowledge my stammered introduction:
      "I've heard a lot about you," "Nothing bad, I hope."
This was one more of those excruciating moments
      Which my father handled with disconcerting tact,
As when he walked into my bedroom without knocking
      A year or two later, and caught me in the act . . .
Drawing on his experience in Circulation,
      Bjorn knew how to talk to my father fair and square,
And they chatted about the weather and my welfare
      At cross purposes, as if neither one were there.
When Bjorn asserted that I showed a lot of promise
      My father commented on the lengthening days,
And told that I had all the makings of a poet,
      Remarked, as of the backward Spring, "It's just a phase."
He was presently to pass a similar judgment
      On what I told him of my emotional bent:
"A period you are passing through—not uncommon—
      "It will go away." But of course it never went.
More realistic, and therefore more pessimistic,
      Bjorn Daj declared my condition congenital
And while I suspected that was rather simplistic,
      At least it implied that it was incurable.
For all the almost universal condemnation
      This statistical abnormality incurred,
I could neither try to deny the diagnosis
      Nor see any necessity for being cured.
Such was the stubborn integrity of my illness

I could hardly conceive what was described as health
In pseudoscientific disapproving sermons
    Perused in the stacks of the library in stealth.
Here I was surprised to find one frivolous title
    Which illustrated a cultural gulf as well,
The French translation of a glum government Survey,
    Ici et là au Canada, Delits Sexuels.

The pretext I devised for being in the basement
    The hours my permissive protector was away
Was an offer on my part to design the backdrop
    For the library's yearly childrens' puppet play.
The head librarian grew puzzled then indignant
    At how long the simple painted scenery took,
When, shirking my two-dimensional childish project,
    I was often as not deep in an adult book.
The result I could no longer delay unveiling
    Was an awful, awkwardly drawn, off-coloured daub,
All too plainly the product of the final minute
    And what Bjorn Daj crudely labelled an off-hand job.
His principal qualification as an expert
    In such matters was the training he liked to tell
Me about, in a juvenile reformatory
    Where he worked as librarian. Heaven or hell
Depended, he said, on your relative position,
    As in any society: all raw recruits
Either submitted or were used against their wishes;
    For a few cigarettes some became prostitutes.
Shocked and titillated, I found my mixed reactions
    As hard to accept as the incredible facts
Of institutional life. Priggishly protesting
    That my heart envisaged no such animal acts,
Instead I expounded my own high-minded hang-ups
    To the only psychologist I cared to trust,
Who sadly shook his head in helpless deprecation,
    Love being so much more a hopeless case than lust.
Perturbed by less solid and ponderable problems
    Than those evidently soluble in the flesh,

April

I pestered Bjorn Daj night and day with stale old chestnuts
    New to me and almost indigestibly fresh.

It seemed that so-called deviant behaviour, whether
    The result of degeneracy or its cause,
An acquired or congential characteristic,
    Was subject to intolerant, repressive laws
In Canada and every English-speaking country,
    Although these were of course selectively enforced.
Heterosexuals suffered less, but they needed
    A special act of parliament to be divorced.
That heretics were still cruelly persecuted
    I found hard to credit in this late age and day,
But whenever I see the headline, *Steambath Raided,*
    I cannot pretend it is no sweat being gay.
Since then the law has somewhat relaxed its full rigour,
    In the case of most consenting adults at least,
And despite the jeremiads of the self-righteous
    Private acts are not so uniformly policed.
But this was a less open and permissive era,
    When to be perverted meant to be circumspect,
While certain secret and inconspicuous signals
    Permitted interested persons to suspect
The truth, particularly in some public places
    Through which I passed in oblivious innocence,
Such as the notoriously busy 'Bus Station
    Which struck me as seedy in no seminal sense.
The sordid, uninviting, and perilous purlieus
    That caution and convenience used to select!
The monuments to self-indulgence and oppression
    Respectability once forced us to erect!
An event that had preordained this paranoia
    Was the tragicomic trial of Oscar Wilde,
Degenerating into farce, like his plays and the
    Fairy stories I found so funny as a child.

If my innocence seems somewhat exaggerated,
    As a collector may exaggerate the cost

Of a worthless object, innocence by its nature
　　Is generally appreciated when lost.
If innocence be relative, and relatively
　　Unimportant, its loss at least seems absolute,
The transmutation irreversible and final
　　From stuck-up virgin to down-to-earth prostitute.
While most of the prostitutes of my slight acquaintance
　　Have been modest and proper almost to excess,
The rather fewer, exclusively female, virgins
　　Were all too shameless in deportment, speech and dress.
As to whether Miss Knight, for instance, was a virgin,
　　I did not at the time give a curious thought,
But judging by her invariable decorum,
　　I am inclined to suspect later she was not.
Bjorn himself, for all his theoretical know-how
　　Had had little or no first-hand experience,
As he wryly confessed, and I of course believed him
　　In the face of the photographic evidence.
Thanks not so much to my youth as to my instinctive
　　Perversity I preserved a virginity
Which I bitterly deprecated as a burden
　　More oppressive than homosexuality,
Another (Bjorn believed) congenital condition,
　　Which while a crime from time to time was not a sin;
Furthermore, he irrelevantly reassured me,
　　I appeared less effeminate than feminine.
Why this seemed at the time plausible or important,
　　Like sex itself is a source of some puzzlement,
As if the vaunted difference between the sexes
　　Were no more than a matter of temperament,
And a man like Hopkins were any the less manly
　　For ending too many lines with feminine feet;
So a female soul inside a masculine body
　　Always struck me as an untenable conceit.
Because I feel comfortable in a kimono
　　Do I become inadequately masculine?
Men were men long before the barbarous invention
　　Of bifurcated dress to hide their manhood in.

Say that I half accepted society's verdict,
    Did it mean that I ought to learn to sew and cook?
If balls were exclusively masculine equipment,
    What was intrinsically feminine in a book?
There is the sexist example of the French language,
    Where *book* is masculine, as everyone recalls,
Though few but francophones are likely to remember
    The gender of *waterfront* or of *waterfalls*.
As to emotional maternal introjection,
    Bjorn Daj was anxious to allay my hopes and fears,
Not being of the pop post-Freudian opinion
    That monopolist mothers manufacture queers.

Like Miss Knight, Daj was (but for quite opposite reasons)
    Inclined to be impatient with my patient love
Of the unattainable, and coarsely suggested
    That the toughest nuts would crack when push came to shove.
Meanwhile he said he knew a promising young fellow
    Encountered on his weekly visit to the 'Y'
Who might be just the ticket. He shewed me his picture.
    Two years older than I, the boy claimed to be 'bi'.
Bjorn Daj was more than willing to set up a meeting
    Between me and this handsome and versatile guy.
After prolonged theoretical preparation
    The crux of the matter lay at my fingertips;
Now the time had come for practical education
    In give-and-take and touch-and-go relationships.
A rendezvous agreed to in the sporting spirit
    Of an arranged royal marriage or a blind date
Soon brought me early to the place of assignation,
    And my prospective partner, as expected, late.
I figured I should recognize him from the picture
    Bjorn had shewn me, but would he look different dressed
For the street in an imitation-leather jacket?
    Self-conscious in my incongruous Sunday best
I felt an understandable last-minute panic—
    What was I going to say to him to begin
With?—as bashful in my tongue-tied anticipation
    As if I had been wearing nothing but my skin.

* * *

Daj played with aplomb the ungrateful role of pander
    (Whom the lover seldom thanks and never forgives),
Lending me the key to his photographic darkroom
    In which to develop our candid negatives,
Hinting that a few shots of us before and after
    Would be one of the procurer's prerogatives.
This bare suggestion, which at first I found quite shocking,
    Might have resulted in a priceless document,
More engaging in retrospect than baby pictures:
    However in the event there was no event.
In April twilight at a designated 'bus-stop
    I awaited my seducer, who never came.
Not having met him in the flesh, after so many
    Years I cannot recollect my intended's name.
Meanwhile Spring, also kept waiting, almost unnoticed
    Had arrived, like puberty heart-breakingly brief,
As if to emphasize my passing disappointment
    And underline my undeniable relief.
Wandering homeward through the germinating landscape,
    My physical innocence stubbornly intact,
After so portentous an overture I wondered
    What—and when—would be the climax of the first act?

MAY DAY

When we were very young, a favourite, forbidden
    Playground was the empty, or rather not yet filled
Flimsy wooden frameworks of half-constructed houses,
    Where the maternal warning that we might be killed
Only added, as in stories, to the adventure
    Of exploring skeletal, perspicuous rooms
Whose predictable future furniture and function
    Lured us careless and incredulous to our dooms,
Which were not to die but to live in just such settings
    Complete with kitchens, bathrooms, living-rooms and halls,
Their airy architecture, to childish eyes, ruined
    By our not being able to see through the walls.

Was one not, at that age or later, as transparent
    As those unfinished buildings, oneself incomplete,
One's character and conscience still under construction,
    The walls of the ego undefined by defeat?
I appeared to myself emotionally naked,
    So defenceless and devoid of any disguise
That a shrewd stranger could see through me in a twinkling
    And read my open secrets in my downcast eyes.
It is not all that uncommon in adolescence,
    This sneaking sensation that one is made of glass;
The Venetian Glass Nephew, by Elinor Wylie,
    Might have described any male member of my class:
Not only transparent but brittle, if unbroken,
    For all their superficial toughness touchy in
So many spots: a sudden awkwardness of manner,
    A sullen scowl or an ingratiating grin.
The limited perspicacity of most adults
    With regard to the painfully perspicuous
Provided our privacy with a partial protection:
    Normal grown-ups, I noticed, seldom noticed us.
My father for example could be unobservant,
    A blindness I am inclined both to praise and blame,

For if he overlooked my childish peccadilloes
    He failed to recognize my change of name,
With which, as in a private rite of confirmation,
    I marked my sense of a mature identity,
My first name like baby clothes outgrown and discarded
    In favour of my second which I felt 'was me'.
As a non-practising Presbyterian Fraser
    (This coincidentally was *his* middle name)
Might frown upon the Romish ritual of passage,
    But had he not in nomenclature done the same?

Teenagers, although they suppose themselves transparent
    To outsiders, to one another seem opaque
As the blinds that are suddenly drawn in their faces,
    Like sleepwalkers, neither sound asleep nor awake.
Which may explain their often off-handed behaviour
    And the peculiarly dumb mistakes they make.
To the many who have practically forgotten
    The outlook of youth, the young are invisible
Rather than transparent, except when too obtrusive
    To be ignored, irritating and risible;
To each other as to themselves they remain deeply
    Significant, at the same time mysterious
And overly familiar, like their changing bodies,
    Their predicaments all painfully serious.
This absence of a sense of humour or perspective
    Renders adolescents ridiculous to those
Who had abandoned the poetry of emotion
    For sober, informative and ironic prose.

One exception to the indifference of adults
    In my experience, my mother, far from blind,
Could not only see through my silent misdemeanours
    But with uncanny penetration read my mind,
With the result that, as I seemed to have no secrets
    From her anyway, I spontaneously told
Her everything before she asked, a candid habit
    I continued until upwards of twelve years old,
When disease, and then death, diverted her attention.

Her posthumous influence dictated my choice
Of chastity, as conscience (or the super-ego)
        Spoke with her quiet, authoritarian voice.
Less censorious, and certainly less maternal,
        Bjorn Daj, too, could read me like an overdue book,
Divining before I told him my disappointment,
        No doubt from my dramatically discouraged look.
"Don't worry," he said, "there will be other occasions.
        You have a lifetime yet, believe it or not.
After the anxiety of anticipation
        There follows the anticlimax of afterthought.
In the path ahead there will be unpleasant patches
        Like this, trying times when there is nothing to do
But endure, obstacles that you cannot get over
        Or under or around but must simply go through."

Just such an ordeal, the celebration of May Day,
        Here traditionally observed not on the first
As elsewhere, but several wearisome weeks later,
        Was of compulsory exercises the worst,
Involving as it did the school-aged population
        In endless rehearsals for an untimely fête—
At least they seemed endless to those who on the sidelines,
        Like me, did nothing for hours on end but wait.
This local tradition was, like everything local,
        After all of ridiculously recent date,
And the primitive symbolism of the maypole
        (Though some prettified ones were erected), ignored
In favour of a display of mass callisthenics
        By which even the young participants were bored.
A far cry from the *Pervigilium Veneris*!
        (Wherein I had not been initiated yet)
With its refrain, *Cras amet qui numquam amavit*,
        And conversely, *Quique amavit cras amet*,
Meaning, in a free if not libertine translation,
        "Whoever has never loved tomorrow will love,
And whoever has loved before will love tomorrow."
        A promise I was properly dubious of,
Seeing there could be no doubt to which category

I belonged, like it or not—see *passim* above.
As it was, not as it were, nothing orgiastic
    Happened during this expurgated Rite of Spring
Save some innocuous infantile Morris dancing
    And incidents of mutinous malingering
Among the older boys as they practised their Swedish
    Drill, of which somehow I could never get the swing.

All the school principals taking it in rotation
    To supervise, this year it was my father's turn,
Making me a private in the paternal army.
    Like L. Junius Brutus he was just but stern,
And would not if necessary have hesitated
    To condemn me to death for talking out of turn,
In order, he would have said, to set an example
    Of perfect parental impartiality;
He must avoid at all costs (to me, of course) any
    Appearance of exceptional leniency.
How I used to envy other pupils their parents!
    Permissive and unpedagogic *hoi polloi*
Whose home life was not an extension of the classroom,
    And for whom an I.Q. test was not a new toy.
Most of my schoolfellows welcomed the preparations
    For May Day as a relief from the old routine,
As they gleefully greeted any interruption
    In the workings of the academic machine;
For despite a high degree of regimentation
    And some intensification of tedium,
They then enjoyed a sort of supervised vacation,
    A foretaste of the summer holidays to come.
I dismissed such freedom as a servile illusion
    And the clubs we were manipulating as dumb
Bells, like most of the boys who clumsily mishandled
    Them, few of whom possessed intelligence as well
As looks and athletic prowess, like Donald Wisdom,
    Being for the most part dumb without being *bel.*

The petty criminals I called contemporaries
    Contemptuously because they were doing time

With me in the Canadian Public School System
    Were the collective victims of white collar crime.
The ennui inseparable from education
    Was justified as a preparation for life,
Whereas for my part I was appalled at the prospect
    Of growing up to a job, a mortgage, a wife,
Whereof I recall a sexist definition
    Overheard during rehearsal in Royal Park,
As 'Something you screw on the bed that does the housework'—
    Like that of sex as 'something you do in the dark.'
A sufficient but not necessary condition
    According to the loose talk I used to eavesdrop
On half accidentally, both ashamed to listen
    And usually too fascinated to stop:
For instance, a boy who claimed to have concentrated
    The light of science on a microscopic drop
Not of pond water but of his own seminal fluid
    (He did not call it that), "to see the tadpoles squirm".
He boasted he had more labwork than he could handle
    As everybody wanted to inspect his sperm.
But if this tad became a successful physician
    (And is any other kind supposed to exist?),
A warm interest in the reproductive system
    Made of every lad a budding specialist.

I was pinning my hopes for May day on the weather,
    Chancy in British Columbia at all times,
Although nobody I knew carried an umbrella,
    As is customary in such pluvial climes.
Anyone who did would have been scorned as a sissy,
    As if he had worn braces instead of a belt.
And was likely to be teased in a mock-toff accent,
    "A bumbershoot, I declare! Afraid you will melt?"
The rainfall that May was a discouraging let-down
    For it dawned persistently and perversely fair.
I prayed the way a heathen might pray for a downpour,
    But heaven appeared indisposed to hear my prayer.
It often rained at night, and sometimes in the morning
    The scowling sky would look fleetingly overcast,

But always when the time came for May Day rehearsal
    The infuriating Pacific storm had passed.

We rehearsed, not in the little park abutting
    The school-yard, our familiar noon-hour stamping ground,
But in a big stadium at a daunting distance,
    Which we were marched to, and when we got there, around.
I once saw a movie of the Nazi Olympics
    Called (unless I'm mistaken) "Triumph of the Will";
As if in immature, amateur imitation
    The spirit of '36 was goosestepping still.
Martial virtues we were being drilled to embody
    Included spunk and guts and vim and grit and pep,
But above all dumb obedience. I was hopeless
    At knee-jerk manoeuvres, and could not keep in step.
Presiding over this unspontaneous circus
    In the place of honour, a prepubescent girl,
The Elected Miss in a school-wide competition,
    Was crowned Queen of the May, a gritty little pearl
Not yet comparable to a titty prune. However,
    This Blessed Damozel, *la demoiselle elue,*
Had only, like her counterpart in far-off London,
    Colourful, ceremonial duties to do.
If she seemed an inadequate stand-in for Venus,
    In whose honour we performed these secular games,
Few of her votaries, vicious prevaricators,
    Had much use for what they dismissively called "dames"—
In the flesh at least, for their bare representation
    On paper appeared another kettle of fish,
To judge by the photographs that were circulated
    Surreptitiously, which aroused a feverish
Interest in the stands that formed the superstructure
    Of the aforementioned large wooden stadium
Where for hours and hours every day we were imprisoned
    Waiting for our minutes out on the field to come.

Need I add that naturally boredom was rampant?
    I tried to dispell mine with a contraband book,
Reading, like talking and smoking, being forbidden.

MAY

All we were supposed to do was sit still and look
At the antics of the innocent May Pole dancers
    And listen to the cacophonous High School band,
Certainly not to examine the filthy pictures
    That were passed with comments from hand to grubby hand.
Absorbed in Biographia Literaria,
    I glanced at one such specimen and passed it on,
A close-up of the feminine genitalia
    Which excited no more reaction than a yawn.
While not unfamiliar with equally gross poses,
    I found the gynecological interest
Of these offensive not by moral but aesthetic
    Criteria: I preferred women fully dressed.
My blasé indifference did not go unnoticed—
    In juvenile circles no deviation does.
"Don't you know the beaver is our national emblem?"
    Sneered one boy no more patriotic than I was.
(One funny thing about hypocrisy in passing:
    The young who indulge in indiscriminate play
Generally make a 'normal adjustment' later;
    It is those who refrain who often turn out 'gay'.)

Chivalrously to my defence came Donald Wisdom,
    Who had hardly spoken a word to me all Spring,
Proclaiming with the conviction of an eye-witness,
    "He doesn't need a snapshot! He's seen the real thing!"
This statement encountered a sceptical reception
    Among our peers. I blushed, but Donald called my bluff.
"Ask him what they were up to in Brad Berry's basement."
    "Oh," someone commented, "that corny old kid-stuff!"
"No, the way I heard it, this time there was a woman . . ."
    An exaggeration: we had been ten years old.
But I wondered where he had got his information,
    For this was one story that I had never told,
Its heroine a forthright undeveloped tomboy
    Who used to join us in what we called 'playing rude';
The flood of puberty to come obliterated
    All details of this voyeuristic interlude,
But I remember my curious disappointment

At female anatomy, which seemed an affront
To my burgeoning sense of the sacred and secret:
    Unlike the boys, she had nothing to show up front.
"That," I expostulated, "was in the Dark Ages—
    At least the basement was dark." This got me a laugh
Which did not diminish my gratuitous standing
    In their eyes, which were glued to the photograph.

What I could not understand was why Donald Wisdom
    Had so suddenly decided to take my side.
For months my mute but unmistakable devotion
    Had been something he used nervously to deride,
Such overtly orientated adulation
    Being a rare exception rather than the rule
In any coeducational institution
    Unlike a segregated British public school.
But could he be feeling not only galled but flattered
    By admiration, however suspect the source?
Incense is always gratifying to an idol
    And even the stars wink in their celestial course.
If I have neglected the object of my worship,
    Which was to constitute the subject of this book,
It is in part because he so seldom responded,
    Beyond an odd word or an even odder look.
That there is no such thing as unrequited friendship
    His unresponsiveness to my overtures of
Friendliness seemed to prove: anything as one-sided
    As my feelings must, unspeakably, be called love.
Don seemed to accept my inevitable presence
    At school, or on the sidelines of whatever game
He starred in with such startling, superior brilliance,
    And sometimes addressed me in passing by my last name
Or once in a blue moon by a sobriquet, namely
    'Shadow', not altogether inappropriate,
In light of the patient fidelity of shadows.
    Such recognition, implying our intimate
Not to say inseparable interconnection,
    Barely acknowledged with an ironic grimace,
Was my reward for months of silent adoration—

But I did not presume to hope for an embrace.
That, or any other form of physical contact
          Was taboo off the ice or playing field or court,
Which besides the manly spirit of competition
          May account for the popularity of sport.
Most Canadian males who consider a handshake,
          Well calibrated as to duration and strength,
The only possible greeting and valediction,
          Hold one another literally at arm's length.
How I envied those in less philophobic cultures,
          The French, the Russian, the American, the Greek,
Where men, like women here, are permitted in public
          To hold hands and to kiss each other on the cheek.
For all my forbidden and informative reading
          And the blatantly hard-core content of my dreams,
My waking desire was for nothing more explicit
          Than a chaste caress, incredible as that seems.
But even of that I was to be frustrated
          By the curious, indeed perverse commonplace
Whereby studs who indulge in hearty hanky-panky
          Shrink from innocent intimacy face to face.
We remained, despite my obsequiousness, strangers,
          As ill-acquainted as Dante and Beatrice.
Nightly I dreamed of unthinkable, nameless favours,
          While daily aspiring not so high as a kiss.
With a shadow, however, I had this in common,
          A faithful attachment, silent but indiscreet;
Almost everywhere he went I was prone to follow,
          Lying figuratively stretched out at his feet,
Animated from time to time by a kind gesture,
          Or banished temporarily by his retreat.
He withdrew now, detonating his verbal bombshell
          Without waiting to hear the sharp laughter explode,
He regained his elevated perch in the bleachers
          Heedless of the small seed of scandal he had sowed.

It came as an irrational humiliation—
          Really a relief, and certainly no surprise—
When on account of my lack of coordination

I was excused from further public exercise
But forbidden to absent myself altogether
    From the arena, in case of unforeseen need.
In the meantime I had no other occupation
    Than being there, not even permitted to read.
It was rather as if a novice in a convent
    Were arbitrarily denied the sacrament,
To which full participation in school athletics
    Counted as a rough secular equivalent.
Disagreeable, even for a disbeliever
    Like me, the sense of being excommunicate
As I watched the elect approach the outdoor altar,
    Not myself the only physical reprobate:
Useless to remind myself that back in the classroom
    I should exact my revenge when, equally bored,
They must sit in an inattentive stupor watching
    Me conjugate irregular verbs on the board.

But boredom was the source of the small, independent
    Stand I took one interminable afternoon
When, seeing no further real reason for my presence,
    I decided to disappear, like Brigadoon.
At the far end of the exercise field my father,
    Visibly mantled with the purple of command,
While busy issuing contradictory orders
    Kept a cold eye on the drop-outs in the grand stand.
Surreptitiously I conned the subversive volume
    Hidden behind an innocuous comic book,
The Birth of Tragedy from the Spirit of Music,
    Knowing full well that the authorities would not brook
Such flagrant, precocious autodidacticism.
    Ironically, while the other kids used to scan
The funny papers under cover of a textbook,
    I camouflaged Nietzsche inside of *Superman.*

Waiting until I saw my father looking elsewhere,
    I rose and closed my book and, unobserved, sneaked out
Behind the bleachers, into a frightening freedom
    Hitherto only heard enviously about.

MAY

I had never in all my years of school played truant,
    Coming from a strict pedagogic family
In which no graver academic misdemeanour
    Compared to the capital crime of truancy;
But now being of the hedonistic opinion
    That one ought to experience life to the hilt,
I ventured into a world of illicit leisure
    And dissipation adulterated by guilt,
Which lay heavy over my impromptu vacation
    As oppressive and crazy as a patchwork quilt.
This seemed all the more depressing in that the weather
    Continued uncharacteristically fine;
Over and above my temporary depression
    The heartless sun had the insouciance to shine.
A literary acquaintance with the pathetic
    Fallacy had already taught me how remote
From real life it is; the unsympathetic heavens
    Infrequently fail to strike a discordant note.

Without anything resembling a destination
    Beyond the aimless need to make good my escape
I lost myself in the uncultivated landscape
    That lay near the heart of our tidy city-scape,
The Central Park of a miniature Manhattan,
    Like that where in later life I dared to digress,
Less dangerous perhaps but no less stimulating
    A paradox: the artificial wilderness,
Celebrated, at least in lurid, local legend
    For ill-defined, unlikely doings after dark,
Although by daylight it would be hard to imagine
    Anywhere more respectable than Royal Park.
Yet I sensed in the most formally laid-out gardens
    A sensual, subtly subversive atmosphere:
Purity might inhabit a hygienic high-rise;
    The carnal seemed naturally incarnate here,
The primal scene, according to the Bible story
    And *Paradise Lost*, of temptation and the fall,
Whether a taradiddle or an allegory,
    The origin of nature's silent, siren call,

Stronger than the noise, diminishing in the distance,
     Of my erstwhile companions' obedient drill.
Then why was I less aware of the fretful pleasures
     Of freedom than of the bitterness of free will?
There were, I discerned, worse things than the blameless boredom
     At which I had chafed in the safety of the stands;
Now with the added burden of conscious wrong-doing
     I discovered the true weight of time on my hands.
Unaccustomed as I was to open rebellion,
     I exaggerated the stature of my crime,
And as thieves are said to squander their ill-got profits,
     I threw away my stolen liberty and time.

Not finding my surroundings conducive to study,
     Except nature study, which I had learned to loathe,
Hardly the kind of park that abounded in benches
     Apart from fallen logs in the rank undergrowth,
Also wishing to put a temporary buffer
     Between myself and a well-deserved dressing-down,
I ventured out of the dim sylvan sanctuary
     Into the civil grid of the surrounding town
Where the street names end in Place and Square and Crescent,
     The geometry of affluence: it was plain
That the inhabitants of avenues were numbered
     Among trespassers in this eminent domain.
As such I felt conspicuous on foot, a prowler
     Through the purlieus of what passed for an upper class,
Faute de mieux, the nouveaux riches of New Westminster,
     At an hour, what's more, when I should have been in class,
In the opinion of the suspicious policeman,
     Frowning as if he had caught me playing a prank,
Who stopped me in one block and asked what I was doing?
     "What does it look like?" I answered, "Robbing a bank?"
Earning myself a thoroughly merited lecture
     On impertinence; but my imminent arrest
On a charge of loitering was changed to a warning,
     While I pretended to look properly impressed,
More abashed, as always, by my own thoughtless back-talk
     Than by its result. How often had I been told

That unthinking winged words would land me in trouble?
  Yet I remained in speech suicidally bold,
At least until the ill-considered shaft departed
  From the bow of my lips, too swift to be recalled
But all too seldom either accurate or pointed
  When it was too late to apologize, appalled
As I was by my brashness. With the question, Whither?
  The perennial problem of the fugitive,
This brief introduction to the life of an outlaw
  Quickly convinced me that it was no way to live.
Knowing of nowhere a delinquent might be welcome,
  Not even under the library's lofty dome,
Clutching the discredited theories of Nietzsche,
  I bent my errant steps towards my lonely home.

When he returned, my father, more in pique than sorrow,
  Inquired crossly where I had spent the afternoon,
And when I told the truth, unable to dissemble,
  Said that I should hear from the proper quarter soon.
In principle he distinguished his role as a parent
  From his duties as a principal, as a rule
Referring to a superior jurisdiction
  The miscreant who went to secondary school.
In the meantime I was neither starved of my supper
  Such as it was, nor packed off untimely to bed,
The postponement of punishment itself a penance
  Intended, I imagine, to augment my dread.

Summoned next morning to the vice principal's office
  During English, for the first time I heard my name
On the P.A. system—like getting in the papers,
  An occasion of ambivalent pride and shame.
As an object of ironic congratulation
  Couched in inarticulate, satirical noise,
I found myself, on first getting into hot water,
  Miraculously, magically one of the boys.
Adolescence, by adult standards nihilistic,
  Has its own unwritten but immutable laws.
Hitherto in the generational class conflict

I had been suspect as a traitor to the cause.
Now our warden received me sternly, as a rebel
      Without a cause, probably without an excuse,
But as a courtesy to a colleague (my father)
      Asked if I had any apology to produce?
When in extenuation I cited my boredom,
      He snorted. "Three years as a prisoner of war
Taught me to appreciate the value of boredom.
      In later life you will find many things a bore."
"So that's why you run this school like a concentration
      Camp, that we may learn to bear the beams of ennui?"
He sighed in despair and dismissed me with instructions
      In future to curb my anarchic levity.

My father welcomed the account of my comeuppance
      With "I told you so," intending to underline
The folly of my misconduct and what a headache
      It was keeping such a troublemaker in line:
A metaphor derived from the scholastic practice
      Of lining students up on the slightest pretext,
While the subjects of this monstrous regimentation
      Respond to the anonymous vocative, "Next!"

May Day came off as planned, the freak weather permitting.
      The elementary school danced, the high school marched,
Like a parody of the Congress of Vienna,
      In their best bibs and tuckers, scrubbed and combed and starched,
Without me. I was sequestrated in the classroom
      By a whim of educational discipline
That rewarded disobedience with a penance
      Too well replicating the original sin.
Thus I had to imagine Don Wisdom resplendent
      In sweat and dust, a paragon among his peers;
I encountered his priggish counterpart in *Phèdre*,
      Read in detention: so much for French Without Tears.

JUNE: D DAY

Our interest, indeed belief in the existence
    Of certain fictional characters, such as God,
Outside their original, literary setting,
    Is a tribute not only to artistic fraud—
What E. M. Forster calls "faking"—but to the reader's
    Naive or knowledgeable gullibility,
Which, not content with Happily Ever After,
    Wants to know the hero's subsequent history,
As if life, which furnishes so few happy endings,
    Could improve upon the false symmetry of art,
Or with its unpredictability and failures
    Had any palatable lesson to impart.

The last stretch between May Day and summer vacation
    At the end of June, was an academic joke;
Discipline relaxed, while our volatile attention
    Dissipated, often literally in smoke.
As I have said, we knew nothing of Maui-Wowie,
    Let alone acid, downers, uppers, smack or speed;
Its use frowned on in school but widespread there as elsewhere,
    Ours was a less illicit but more noxious weed.
We could not look forward to a formal commencement;
    Such ceremonies were less common in those days.
The eventual goal of High School Graduation
    Seemed far off when in scholastic medias res.
At the most there might be an ultimate assembly
    Where prizes and platitudes were handed out—
I would get my first, for "academic achievement"—
    But nothing, we complained, worth writing home about.
Otherwise the pedagogic life-support system
    Simply stopped, like a clock, from one day to the next,
A prospect to delight most of my fellow-students
    Which left me feeling inexplicably perplexed.
While for once in class I was rarely reprimanded
    For reading things thought unsuitable for my age,

The alternative reading of an open window
    Solicited my concentration from the page
Toward a punctuated line of pointed poplars
    Rhythmical in their syncopated foliage,
At the edge of the playing field whose printed surface
    Recalled scores of athletic contests stamped in mud
Soon erased by an annual precipitation
    Which approached that recorded just before the Flood.
Here the querulous voices of quarrelsome children,
    A cacophonous but enthusiastic choir,
Performed with the shrill spontaneity of birdsong
    The counterpoint of competition and desire.
I did not, unlike most of my restless coevals,
    Particularly want to run amuck outside;
It was an ill-defined, indefinable freedom
    For which, without knowing precisely why, I sighed.
As if in spite of my sedentary aversion
    To the Spartan cult of exercise and fresh air,
I sensed that something more fundamental than baseball
    Was going on quite openly somewhere out there.
Returning with an abridged sigh to *Death in Venice*
    I found in the northern nostalgia for the South
The same tendency as mine to see the whole summer
    In the shape of an exquisitely modelled mouth.
Don Wisdom, in profile between me and the window,
    Flattered but flustered by my worshipful regard,
Fidgetted, his wary glances in my direction
    Beautifully maintaining his ironic guard.
As the last day of school drew near we drew no closer,
    For hours of each day separated by the aisle;
His random asides were delivered in a whisper,
    As infrequent and noncommital as his smile.
Apart from that there was plainly nothing between us
    Except my idolatrous stare and his good looks;
Otherwise we inhabited different planets,
    He the athletic sphere, and I the world of books.

Then one morning in early June his place was empty
    At roll call. He was so often absent or late

On one trumped-up, transparent pretext or another
    That I did not at once begin to speculate
On his whereabouts or worry about his welfare,
    Nor can I claim to have had a presentiment
Of disaster, till Miss MacColl made the announcement
    That Don had met with a near-fatal accident
Yesterday afternoon, delivering his papers,
    When he was hit by a car and thrown off his bike.
Now he lay in hospital where, when out of danger,
    She reassured us, she was certain he would like
Visitors. In the meantime she raised a subscription
    To send our fallen playfellow a get-well card.
She had hardly hinted how badly he was injured,
    And I prayed that he not be permanently scarred.
If this sounds somewhat cynical and superficial,
    As if Wisdom's beauty were no more than skin deep,
It seemed the embodiment of the bedtime story
    I used to tell myself before falling asleep . . .
Don Wisdom being a popular, all-round athlete,
    A suitable card was selected, signed, and sent;
And as soon as I heard that he was convalescent,
    Without waiting for an invitation, I went
To see him. Accustomed to visiting my mother
    In hospital as I was, this felt different.
In the first place, I had to travel to Vancouver
    General, a good hour away by tram or 'bus.
There I knew he had been taken for special treatment
    Unavailable here, and thither amorous
Friendship emboldened me devotedly to follow,
    As if distance were all that now divided us.
The still waters of love, while polluted by pity,
    Did not therefore become brackish or run less deep.
Having myself lately been in some need of comfort,
    I held gratuitous commiseration cheap,
Indeed in the case of young Wisdom, all but worthless,
    Since he seemed to have been forgotten in a week
By his pals on the playground, cruelly confirming
    Time's indifference to a beautiful physique.
Then who could have foreseen he would not be forgotten

By me after a lapse of more than thirty years?
Remembered and reanimated by the magic
    Of language? In memory nothing perseveres
Like unrequited desire, refrigerated
    Among frozen aspirations and freeze-dried tears.

Hitherto I had never made the return journey
    From our town to the big city and back alone,
And doing so now I felt, like the scruffy suburbs
    Through which I passed in between, how fast I had grown.
Like the overnight defloration of the country
    (A commonplace of our culture) by urban sprawl,
One devastating side-effect of education
    Is this unevenly developed interval.
If childhood in romantic retrospect seems rural,
    Forever green, unspoilt, spontaneous, and
The habitat of mankind is the grown-up city,
    Adolescence is a spotty no man's land,
Through which I sped with the impatience of a Greyhound
    But still slower than desire, to the bedside of
My unconscious love who, whatever his condition,
    Was (or so I assumed) unconscious of my love.

The hospital room in which I found him was private,
    But I barely recognized him, so pale and still
He lay, an agent willy-nilly now a patient,
    Wrapped in the pallid passivity of the ill,
No longer that incessantly active, quicksilver
    Moving picture of health and youth and energy,
But an inert and lifeless yet nonetheless lifelike
    Breathtakingly perfect ivory effigy,
White on white, shrouded by a sheet, his broken body
    A slight eminence in the hospital bed.
I stared, equally immobilized, in the doorway
    Till the statue miraculously moved its head
Signalling, as in A Winter's Tale, the unlooked-for
    Return of the lost and revival of the dead.
His smile was warm but wan, a slight grimace of welcome
    Discouraging my words of sympathy before

I could utter them, as he ruefully received me
    As his first extrafamilial visitor.
When I asked how he felt, the conventional question
    Literally meant, was he feeling any pain?
On the contrary, he assured me that he felt nothing
    From the waist down, and feared he never would again—
Not only never walk but never play ice hockey
    Or lacrosse or baseball, or dance, or run a race.
My impulse, perhaps excessively empathetic,
    Was to wish, sincerely, that I were in his place:
After all, my interests were far from athletic,
    My habits already sedentary enough;
I could read and write as easily in a wheelchair . . .
    But I murmured noncommitally, "Gee, that's tough."
Brushing aside such stilted expressions of pity,
    He returned to the matter of the physical
With a plethora of anatomical detail
    Epidemic among patients in hospital.
No more disinterested than a jailhouse lawyer
    Whose early release is his (often unpaid) fee,
The heightened morbid sensitivity of illness
    Makes everybody *un medecin malgré lui,*
Describing the most extraordinary symptoms
    With pathological and uninfectious glee.
So he told me exactly where his back was broken,
    And his spinal cord severed, thus rendering him
Something he mispronounced as a "parapelegic",
    And that his chances for recovery were slim.
His damaged lower limbs were bandaged like a mummy,
    Uncannily static beneath the placid sheet,
As dumb as an abandoned ventriloquist's dummy
    Discarded in disgrace and speechless in defeat.

He spoke with bitterness rather than resignation—
    It was too early and he much too young for that—
As if, hitherto living in and for the body,
    He found that his partner had gone and left him flat.
I tried to remind him of certain compensations—
    My only attempt at consolation—in vain:

What, compared to the loss of function and sensation,
    Was the fact that he was alive and not in pain?
I spoke airily of intellectual pleasures,
    But he muttered, "That's o.k. for you, you're a brain."
I refrained from pointing out that in his condition
    He could do no better than become one as well,
For the first effect of any bodily breakdown
    Is the extent to which it compells us to dwell
In the flesh. The basis of spiritual freedom
    Rests on a hidden bedrock of physical health,
In the same way that economic independence
    Reposes on a foundation of unearned wealth.
Instead, an inkling of the impotence of pity
    To satisfy or even comprehend his need
Unmanned me so that all I could manage to stammer
    Was, "Would you like me to bring you something to read?"
He laughed, "I guess I'll have to catch up on my reading."
    Poor boy! born before the diffusion of the tube
Made every erstwhile participant an onlooker,
    And every pseudo-intellectual a boob.
Marvelling how anybody could get through even
    Half-an-hour without reading matter of some kind,
Much as I sympathized with Don Wisdom's affliction,
    My own anxieties were otherwise defined.
I would much rather lose the use of all members,
    I vowed short-sightedly at the time, than go blind,
But blindness itself would not be such a disaster,
    I thought, as the penultimate loss, of my mind.
I was of course not only naive but wrong-headed.
    There is no hierarchy of unhappiness;
All disabilities seem total at the moment
    When one can discern no distinction in distress.
Topsy-turvy rebellious elements take over
    As in the collapse of the body politic
Where any subversion of the established order
    Prompts one to diagnose society as sick.

I did not communicate these confused reflections,
    If they occurred to me at the time, which I doubt,

JUNE

Only protesting with a pretense of conviction,
    "Before you realize, you'll be up and about."
He shook his head with the infinite pessimism,
    So absolutely unanswerable, of youth,
And sighed. So did I, ashamed of my lie, since silence
    Seemed the only honest alternative to truth.
When on a reckless yet irresistible impulse
    I reached for his hand as it lay outside the sheet,
He moved it aside, as a player might a chessman.
    "Would you like me to come again?" "That would be neat."

So I returned, not only the first but the only
    Of his schoolmates to visit Don in hospital,
Most normal adolescents avoiding affliction
    Like the plague, their instinct healthily animal.
While his recovery was painful, slow and partial—
    As incomplete, indeed, as his paralysis—
Insofar as he grew stronger he grew more lonely,
    Like the victim of some unfeeling prejudice.
For if rich and poor belong to separate races,
    The variant species of the ill and well
Have disparate tastes, vocabularies and customs,
    Different temperatures and a funny smell.
I was far from feeling an attraction to sickness
    As such, having admired him before he fell ill,
But the aftermath of his accident created
    A social vacuum I felt privileged to fill.
Formerly orbited by admirers and rivals,
    He had shone as unapproachable as the sun;
Now in his eclipse, though nowhere near his setting,
    He had become accessible to anyone
Prepared, like me, to take compassionate advantage
    Of his decline. Was I wrong to want to replace
Satellites whose reprehensible dereliction
    Left him spinning alone in empty inner space?
Was I no better than an emotional vampire,
    Feeding on weakness like the newsreel camera?
If so, my victim, far from resenting my visits,
    Clutched at them like a drowning man grasping a straw.

Not that in my tacit but obvious devotion
    There was anything hollow, frivolous or weak!
Throughout the period of his recuperation
    I proved it by going to see him twice a week,
After school, as long as school continued in session,
    And more often during the summer holiday.
Had the 'bus fare been less or my allowance larger,
    I should gladly have made the journey every day.
As it was, my father thought my visits too frequent,
    Believing as he did in nothing to excess,
Especially overt expressions of affection.
    He wished I would talk about my pal's progress less.
It was not as if I wanted to be a doctor,
    Let alone, heaven forbid! a practical nurse.
This brought up the vexatious problem of my future,
    Which should be put on a firmer footing than verse;
Than an eminently respectable profession
    Like medicine he thought that I might do much worse.
In the absence of such intention, my attendance
    At a sick bed struck him as morbid and perverse.
Bjorn Daj, who was in principle more sympathetic
    To the nature of my attachment, criticised
A passion that must prove frustrating and one-sided
    With one of the partners partially paralyzed
And thus to all intents and purposes a eunuch,
    Unable, however touched, to reciprocate—
Though according to a book I read in the basement,
    Kama Sutra, eunuchs were hardly celibate.
Would it, I asked, be any more fruitless than thinking
    Continually of those who are truly straight?
Bea Knight on the other hand, making a novena
    For Don's miraculous cure, praised the pure of heart
Like me, who performed the corporal works of mercy
    In which carnality could play so little part.

Yet in the course of further visits I marvelled
    How what flesh I glimpsed, far from beginning to waste
Away, regained weight, resilience, tone, and colour,
    As his body hypertrophied above the waist.

Vainly demonstrating his daily exercises
    For the development of shoulder, chest, and arms,
While exciting my praise for his heroic efforts
    He made me deplore the coarsening of his charms,
As I observed with dismay his metamorphosis
    Into a caterpillar, from the butterfly
He used to be before his fall, a sluggish process
    I was both revolted and fascinated by.
His face, too, in time, though this might have been expected
    With age, lost some of its previous pulchritude,
In part perhaps because he adopted a crew-cut.
    For the rest, I never again would see him nude.
Suffering, which is said to refine and enoble
    By some mysterious alchemy, and to teach
So much, while it did not debase or make him stupid,
    Subtly rendered him coarser in features and speech.
As if in inverse indeed ironic proportion
    To his potential to enjoy life to the full,
His language became almost painfully explicit.
    Yet for me his beauty remained unspeakable.
The very lack of such varied topics of discourse
    As make up intelligent adult intercourse
Condemned us to the few subjects we had in common—
    Hackneyed, largely inaccurate hearsay, of course—
Or often stranded us in an embarrassed silence
    Of which we were ill equipped to explore the source.

Thus one visit tended to blend into another
    Till the long-anticipated, triumphal day
When Don graduated from his bed to a wheelchair,
    In which for want of a miracle he would stay.
Tantalized, as in school, by the view from the window—
    Summer, attended by delightful scents and sounds—
He pestered his physician till he got permission
    For me to take him out in the hospital grounds.
I found him, on the day of this momentous outing,
    For the first time since the disaster fully dressed,
Seated in the mobile steel-and-leather contraption,
    His sole means of self-locomotion for the rest

Of his life, his legs now obviously redundant
    In neatly pressed slacks, and his Herculean chest
Distending the taut material of his t-shirt.
    Like all expeditions this was to be a test
Not only of our strength and skill in navigation
    But of tolerance for—and of—the world outside.
At his back I assumed my appointed position
    As footman, and we took each other for a ride,
He spinning the wheels energetically forward
    With his hands, which would become both calloused and large,
I steadily and unnecessarily pushing
    Behind the burnished throne he sat in like a barge.
With time this ongoing cooperative effort,
    The unique outlet for my unacknowledged love,
Came to provide its approximate consummation
    When, as Bjorn Daj had predicted, push came to shove.
Descending in an elevator to the basement,
    I began to appreciate what unawares
I had taken for granted, a freedom of movement
    Hitherto uncomplicated by flights of stairs.
The world, perceived from the perspective of a wheelchair,
    When not hopelessly inaccessible, is flat,
The ups and downs that chart pedestrian existence
    Reduced to a two-dimensional habitat.

Exiting through the ground floor Emergency Entrance,
    We emerged into the inviting afternoon,
The tepid temperature and watery sunshine
    Of an uncertain British Columbian June.
The hospital, therapeutically situated
    Amid graded, gravel paths, grass, and flower beds,
Was topped by the tall shaft of an incinerator
    Polluting the atmosphere far above our heads.
This no longer provoked the guilt-stricken recognition
    It might imaginatively a few months back,
Its phallic shape as well as crematory function
    Overshadowed by the matter-of-fact smoke stack.
Under that silently active man-made volcano
    I parked the wheelchair by a rusty rustic bench

Where we might catch our breath in comparative private
    Apart from passersby and the pervasive stench.
Of course there were other scents in the perfumed garden,
    But even the chimney's insalubrious reek
Seemed preferable to the smell of disinfectant
    And anaesthetic in which he was bathed all week.
Impatiently he demanded the cheap tobacco
    And cigarette papers that, as asked, I had brought,
Paraphernalia the patient was forbidden,
    Certain to be confiscated if he were caught.
Odd, how one is considered too young for some pleasures,
    Yet never, self-evidently, too young for pain!
Suffering requires no age of consent. However
    His parents, as he described them, seemed more humane.
Overwhelmed by a guilty sense of helpless pity,
    This well-meaning couple, whom I had not yet met,
Refused their battered and badly-spoilt baby nothing.
    "The other day Dad offered me a cigarette,"
He boasted, "And would have left me the whole darn package
    Only some dumb nurse would have taken it away."
Smoking in those days was condemned as a bad habit
    And not as hazardous to our health, as today.
But anything bad was, naturally, unhealthy
    At our age, especially in the hospital
When certain drugs, with their unsuspected potential,
    Had not begun to be called recreational,
With the legally unavailable exception
    Of any other brand than rubbing alcohol.
Doubtless Don would have asked me to be his bootlegger—
    Parental indulgence had its limits—but I
Was too young for the Government Liquor Commission,
    And afraid to raid my father's meagre supply.
As he rolled us cigarettes (a manual talent
    In which he plainly took understandable pride,
And one which has enjoyed a surprising revival
    In recent decades), he unsuccessfully tried
To teach me how to roll them too, our present laughter
    Occasioned by being alive, young, and outside.
Delighting in the simple-minded fact of being—

No longer such a push-over as once it seemed
In prelapsarian days when living was easy,
      Unlike nowadays—only now and then he dreamed
Dog-like, of running, jumping, or sinking a basket,
      Waking to the knowledge he never would again,
As if the condition of his dejected members
      Still came as a shock to his hyperactive brain.
He might have agreed with Andersen's little mermaid
      That walking would be worth any amount of pain.
Then he described other, indescribable visions
      That haunted and taunted him nearly every night,
Such as enlighten any healthy adolescent,
      Now to him as infeasible as dreams of flight.

If I hesitated to tell him of the torments
      I had incurred during those wasted months when I
Had devoted myself to rigid self-denial,
      It was because he now had nothing to deny.
It seemed as if our conversations alternated
      Between his lamentably chaste and static state
And those joys that he thought I tended to disparage
      And which I thought he was prone to exaggerate.
Of the accident itself he spoke very little,
      Or of the nameless hit-and-run driver involved:
His life had been ruined by a person or persons
      Unknown, and the crime remained for ever unsolved.
Instead, he asked me an unanswerable question
      As we sat there smoking like blazes in the sun,
Namely, the reason I came to see him so often.
      "It's nice of you, but it can't be very much fun."
With the daring of despair I mumbled, "I love you,"
      An avowal that should not come as a surprise
In light of my obvious long-standing devotion.
      "Don't be dumb," he snorted, "Guys can't love other guys."
When I cited the more notorious examples
      From my researches, he incredulously smiled
As if possessed of superior information.
      "You mean," he capped my catalogue, "like Oscar Wilde?"
Strange to relate, this hoary Victorian scandal

Had not been laid to rest generations before,
And the flamboyant figure of the protomartyr
       Formed a permanent fixture of oral folklore.
For this I suppose I ought not to have been sorry.
       The sentimental author of The Happy Prince
Though unhappy, made a less sinister role model
       Than certain gay criminals celebrated since,
As it was his misplaced love for Lord Alfred Douglas
       (Whom my beloved, to judge by the photographs,
Was much lovelier than), that occasioned his downfall,
       And not the riff-raff with whom he was tried for laughs.
I outlined my purely theoretical knowledge
       Without going into details: these he had heard
Enough of already otherwise to consider
       Homosexuality a four-letter word;
And as for my demanding no gratification,
       That he dismissed incredulously as absurd,
Being of the not yet fashionable opinion
       That no homosexual persons, only acts
Exist, a pragmatic oversimplification
       That in my case did not exactly fit the facts.
Unfazed by the symptoms of my infatuation
       He had obdurately refused to understand
Their implication; but whatever my intentions,
       He did not reject my attentions out of hand.
In the first place (and here I could have no illusions)
       I was not only his best but his only friend;
In the second—I am not sure there was a second.
       Friendship must remain not a means but a dead end.
That there could be no question of reciprocation
       He did not need to tell me; I already knew,
Had he wanted he could not perform those perversions
       Which he expressed such a hearty aversion to,
Sufficiently informed by vernacular hearsay
       That *he* could enlighten *me* as to what queers do . . .
I hastened to reassure him that I expected
       Nothing like that—indeed, nothing at all, from him.
He chuckled, "A good thing you're so fucking high-minded,
       Otherwise you'd be out of luck!" The jest was grim,

158

But I shuddered at the cynical carnal knowledge
    That, admittedly secondhand, could lightly cloak
The most delicate and desperate declaration
    In the cast-off rawness of a locker-room joke.
Although I was shocked and hurt I could hardly marvel:
    To one of his age and nation and sex and class
Such a confession as mine must be more upsetting
    Than any speechless, straightforward physical pass.
For one thing, love will never take no for an answer,
    Though it disclaims any notion of quid pro quo,
And while the other is over with when it is over,
    It is not the habit of true love to let go.
Who knows if my friend had proved a mite more forthcoming,
    His body less backward, his tastes less hard-and-fast,
Provided such simple, sensual satisfaction
    As the flesh can offer, how long my love would last?
Content, *faute de pire*, with verbal communication,
    Hoping to catch him in emotional undress,
I inspected in vain his truculent expression
    For a fugitive hint of grateful tenderness;
Meanwhile our preliminary negotiations,
    Unlike haphazard chit-chat, continued to move
In concentric circles like a gramophone record,
    Deeper and deeper in the same eternal groove.
Don manifested a sort of tolerant boredom
    Like that which the mention of poetry inspired
As so much high-flown, incomprehensible nonsense.
    "All right," he yawned, "Take me in now, I'm getting tired."

Wheeling him back from our inconclusive engagement
    In which most of my pipe dreams had gone up in smoke,
I took consolation if not unfair advantage
    From the thought of the wheel of which I was a spoke,
For like a spoke I kept eccentrically returning
    To the turning point where all revolutions start,
All the while patiently, imperceptibly moving
    Forward the invalid vehicle of the heart.

JULY: INDEPENDENCE DAY

The wheel of the law, so liberally lubricated
 With human, and subhuman, blood and sweat and tears,
Supporting the triumphal car of evolution
 Rolled inexorably forward. Weeks became years
(Or so it seemed at the time): in life's rearview mirror
 As in Genesis millennia shrink to days;
The events of that epochal summer blur into
 One another under the heading, Holidays.
The distinction between holiday and vacation
 Being more than merely a matter of extent,
Involves differing degrees of anticipation
 And, eventually, of disillusionment.
In actuality neither endless nor empty,
 The long vacation was often chilly and damp.
Considered too young for even part-time employment
 And too old or unsociable for summer camp,
What my contemporaries welcomed as a promise
 I saw with infinite misgivings as a threat,
And having seen the boys of summer in their ruin
 Decided I was not ripe to be ruined yet.

On my way home one afternoon from bedside duty
 I was trying to read aboard the bumpy 'bus
When a boy in Grade Nine I knew by reputation
 And sight sat down beside me, accosting me thus:
"You know, you'd look so much cuter without your glasses.
 But don't I know you from somewhere? No, let me guess . . ."
His clean-cut, almost too photogenic appearance
 Belied his unblushing mannered outrageousness,
Arousing in me contradictory emotions,
 A sneaking sympathy and bewildered disgust.
Too naive and nearsighted to notice his make-up,
 I found him too precious for an object of lust.
His extravagant vocabulary and gestures,
 Plucked eyebrows, flexible wrist, wanton leer and lisp

Had earned him the glamourous sobriquet of "fairy",
    That is, a sort of sexual will-'o-the-wisp.
Notwithstanding my perhaps mistaken presumption
    That in any case here I risked no rude rebuff,
I discovered one definition of perversion,
    Rejecting that which was not hard-to-get enough.
Nor was I prepared to be any more responsive
    To the curious and conspiratorial way
In which he extracted my inoffensive secret.
    "A doll, of course, but you're wasting your time, I'd say.
Wasn't he badly crippled in some ghastly crack-up?
    Besides, no one that butch could possibly be gay.
Not that I couldn't tell you a few funky stories
    Out of school. No, I like my men in one hunk . . ."
In his mouth the English tongue, already emphatic
    Enough, rhythmically and dramatically rose and sunk.
"Anyway personally I prefer them rather
    Older—I haven't stooped to rob a cradle yet . . ."
He might have inverted Gide's indignant disclaimer
    To, "Je ne suis pas péderaste, je suis tapette."
To hear him tell it, there was one distinct advantage
    To being obvious, even a laughing-stock:
"If you want to attract the right kind of attention
    Along with the wrong, honey, you got to use shock
Tactics." The members of certain exotic species
    Flaunting their colours, gaudy birds and butterflies
Also jeopardise themselves for the sake of mating.
    As he put it smugly, "It pays to advertise."
He regaled me with lurid tales of supine conquest
    Meant to excite envy, which they might have done if
I had a single envious bone in my body.
    "Nowadays the competition is pretty stiff.
You know the old saying, yesterday's trade, tomorrow's
    Competition?" This hinted we were hand in glove,
But I supposed trade was a common euphemism
    For the funny business he was so boastful of.
In fact I had understood no more than a fraction
    Of his allusive (and elusive) sure-fire slang,
Yet I sensed that his questionable subject matter

Was something of which I wanted to get the hang.
Speaking neither in the polysyllabic Latin
    Language of the learned treatises I had read,
Nor in the frank, monosyllabic Anglo-Saxon
    Lingo of our male contemporaries, instead
He spun a tantalizing web of innuendo,
    And I must say I hung on every word he said.
The conversation, fundamentally one-sided—
    What did I have in the way of experience
To contribute?—presumed not mutual but common
    Interests belied by my wide-eyed innocence.
For this monologue, not only shameless but boastful,
    Presupposed in the interlocutor a bent
Unconscious, unavowed, suppressed or sublimated,
    But not in the last analysis different.
Without acknowledging my awed ejaculations
    He sometimes cast me a sidelong quizzical look
Wickedly estimating how much I would swallow
    But never glancing at the title of the book
On my lap, a turgid interminable novel.
    I supposed that he did not find much time to read
With his multifarious affairs. One so oral
    Must find the written word insipid stuff indeed.
But now I remembered overhearing my father
    Who as principal had once failed him in Grade Five
Exclaiming in exasperation that he lacked the
    "Commonsense to keep a canary bird alive."
The comparison was undeniably striking:
    With the shrillest glissando I had ever heard,
He had the unnatural-looking yellow plumage
    And the flighty volubility of that bird.
A sudden flicker of suspicious recognition
    Made him demand, "Is your old man Old Man Hine?"
(Were intelligence instrumental in achieving
    One's objective, his was superior to mine.)
I confessed to the discreditable connection
    That had plagued me throughout my scholastic career.
"Well, I never!" he crowed, demonstrably delighted,

"Wait till I tell them the old bugger's son is queer."
When I resented this gratuitous assumption—
    What had I said or done to give myself away?—
I guessed that he was one for whom the opposite sexes
    Were not male and female but rather "straight" and "gay".
Had I betrayed myself by the tell-tale attention
    I paid his tall tales? Normally, except in bed,
If he kept up this lady-like loverly chatter
    His casual partners no doubt would cut him dead.
Was this an example of the mythical instinct
    Whereby we are said to identify our kind?
Like certain nocturnal, winged, ephemeral insects
    Who find each other across great distances, blind?
If so, I was sorry that such a useful talent
    Did not seem to be universally innate,
Since I tended to be unerringly attracted
    To an obviously unattainable mate.
I am ashamed to admit I, too, was embarrassed
    In public by this happenstance companionship,
And wanted to deny, as I had to another
    Compromising chance acquaintance, that I was hip.
Instead I observed brightly pointing out the window,
    "O look, isn't that a new Safeway going up?"
At which my fellow traveller knowingly tittered,
    "Don't you believe it! There's no safe way going up!"
Forced to laugh, though I did not find this very funny,
    For fear my more experienced mentor might scoff,
I excused myself long before my destination
    With a whopper: "So long. This is where I get off."
I stumbled off the 'bus in the middle of nowhere—
    And yet everywhere is somewhere, like it or not,
Just as everybody is nominally someone,
    Like that nobody whose name I promptly forgot.
But here, whatever its metaphysical status,
    Seemed an unfamiliar and god-forsaken spot.
I found myself in that dilapidated landscape
    I had sniffed at in transit: overgrown plots
In a wasteland without streetlights or signs or sidewalks

Interspersed with raw bungalows on bulldozed lots.
If this rape of the rural scene was reminiscent
    Of recent verbal inroads on my innocence,
It showed me how vulnerable the state of nature
    Is to civilization and its malcontents.
But be that as it may, my immediate problem
    Was to find my way home alone on foot without
A precise sense of my whereabouts, map or compass,
    Or much homing instinct. Looking up and about
At the indifferent but far from distant mountains
    I met the old glacial, lofty stoney look
That had chilled and intimidated me since childhood.
    No turning for guidance to my library book,
Despite its misleading title, *Look Homeward, Angel*;
    I guessed at every direction that it was wrong,
Furthermore I did not have enough nerve to hitchhike,
    But waited for the next Greyhound to come along.

Those two elements of the picturesque in nature
    Usually sundered, the mountains and the sea,
Are to be found cheek by jowl in my native province,
    Often called for that reason Beautiful B.C.
On licence plates and elsewhere. This juxtaposition
    Of the vertical and the horizontal, land
And water, the hard-edged and the impressionistic
    Sometimes impressed me as monotonously grand.
Brought up as I was in an out of doors museum,
    I envied those born and bred in Saskatchewan
(As I might have been) their extensive empty vistas,
    For the sublime in time comes to inspire a yawn.
The mountains, albeit more conspicuous features,
    In practice proved less accessible than the beach,
Where the ocean, invisible and omnipresent,
    Lurked often out of sight but never out of reach.
The vaguest of outlines in all but splendid weather,
    The heights appeared remote and forbidding to climb,
So, though the local waters were too cold for bathing,
    Our orientation was mainly maritime.
As a child I built sandcastles below high water

Line, resigned to their overthrow by tide and time,
Rarely waded out waist deep in the frigid breakers
    (Which may explain why I never learned how to swim),
And confronted in the echoing, foetid bathhouse
    Previews of the members-only horseplay of gym.
When our family expeditions to the seashore
    Expired with my mother, a further painful change
Of scene, Fraser's idea of a Sunday outing
    Meant a drive through the foothills of the Coastal Range.
I may be forgiven the fanciful equation
    Of my father with such petrific scenery,
Admirable, aloof and stern, and of my mother
    With the generous, shapeless, all-embracing sea.
The backgrounds sentimentally associated
    With my characteristic memories of each
Contrast out of focus snapshots of Fraser Canyon
    With wishy-washy watercolours of a beach
In Stanley Park, a favourite spot for a picnic,
    Which mother conceived of as a portable feast,
In addition to the usual cold collation
    Including one hearty, heavy hot dish at least.
In that artificial Arcadia or Eden
    On the verge of Vancouver that was Stanley Park,
We were permitted to frolic only by daylight.
    Dark as the hints of what went on there after dark
Were the doings themselves, until I was enlightened,
    Indeed electrified, by certain lurid scrawls
And anatomical sketches that decorated
    At that time the park's public lavatory walls.
Loose as my grasp was of this new technical jargon,
    As of the acts which it was designed to depict,
Even as a pretty precocious prepubescent
    My private carnal curiosity was pricked.
Others may have picked up more first-hand information
    From hearsay and trial-and-error than I did
From such proto-pornography, but it fixated
    Forever my inhibited, literate Id,
Leaving me with a sneaking suspicion that under

J U L Y

The sunlit Sunday surface of the man-made maze
Of trails interpenetrating the virgin forest
    A wicked world lay in wait for such careless strays
As I; and though I never encountered the perverts
    I was warned of (save myself) in the undergrowth,
I looked forward to my sylvan seduction someday
    With apprehension and anticipation both,
Though I should have run headlong from any seducer
    And regretted it later; from Siwash Rock
To Lumberman's Arch all the landmarks of my boyhood,
    Lost Lagoon and English Bay, even Taplow Walk
Are impregnated with the ambiguous flavour
    That attaches to any leftover of wild
Life artificially preserved within the city,
    Sacred to nature-lover, criminal and child,
Exploration of which on my own was forbidden
    During my mother's lifetime, like so many things
Enjoyed by less sheltered and obedient children,
    The perils of the playground: see-saws, slides, and swings.

Although our trips to Stanley Park were interrupted
    By my mother's death, I grew if anything more
Sensitive to her well-intended prohibitions.
    Temptation presented itself as the foreshore
Of a fascinating, unfathomable ocean
    Whose enticing surface conceals treacherous deeps;
As I waded I felt an undertow of longing
    For this fabulous secret only the sea keeps.
Taught childishly to eavesdrop on The Unpolluted
    By pressing a convoluted shell to my ear,
I came to harbour a solipsistic suspicion
    That my own tidal blood was all that I could hear.
Those who grow up beside a large body of water
    Grow accustomed to views both vague and grandiose
And find the prospects of life inland claustrophobic,
    Unable to focus on anything up close.
A special brand of luxurious melancholy,
    A wistful questioning of life's ultimate worth,

Always haunted me on the edge of the Pacific
    With its sense of being at the ends of the earth.

Told now to turn my back on this terminal question
    Mark, and forbidden to visit my mother's grave,
Estranged from the fluid elements for a season,
    I plunged into sorrow as if under a wave.
Sometimes one of Fraser's topographical namesakes,
    Valley or Canyon, precipitated a drive,
Itself a change from the down-to-earth interurban
    We had always taken when mother was alive.
Father was already shopping for a replacement,
    Unable to contemplate existence alone,
And in the course of his courtly old-fashioned courtships
    I was often conscripted as a chaperone.
As an incurable monogamist, or rather
    A serial polygamist most of his life,
He exaggerated my need for a stepmother
    As an excuse for his search for a second wife.
Needless to say, my wishes were never consulted,
    Otherwise, I should have been the first to decline
The very idea of a surrogate mother,
    Following the loss of such a mother as mine.
Guessing that resistance, not only worse than useless,
    Might strain a relation already sorely frayed,
For the sake of father's peace of mind I consented
    To go along with his uxorious charade.
The most promising applicants for the position
    Were as different as two schoolteachers could be.
The first, Margery, whom I dubbed The Merry Widow,
    Tried to enlist me in a cosy conspiracy,
And wooed me with would-be-flattering small attentions
    In a wasted campaign to win me to her side,
Overestimating my influence with Fraser
    Who sighed for a somewhat less high-spirited bride,
For suddenly from one week to the next she vanished,
    Never to be seen, heard of, or mentioned again.
When questioned, father's short, indignant explanation

Shocked me; he found out that she was "seeing other men."
His attitude seemed an unenlightened example
    Of heterosexual male jealousy,
Which may be observed in several other species
    Where females are treated as private property.

For The Merry Widow's more successful successor,
    As strait-laced and tight-lipped as *she* was fast and loose,
But, like her and almost all of father's acquaintance,
    A school-marm, I for my part had rather less use,
Nicknaming her, mistakenly, The Iron Maiden:
    I soon found out that she was made of sterner stuff
Under her steely exterior. There is nothing
    Tougher or more tenacious than a piece of fluff.
Not that she was what you might call high-flown or flighty.
    My father's age, for twenty-odd years she had taught
Primary School, where contacts with "the little people"
    Had infantilized her habits of speech and thought.
By all Canadian standards a perfect lady,
    Dressed winter and summer in tailored pastel tweeds,
And furthermore all too plainly a maiden lady,
    She had no experience of masculine needs,
To which she reacted with an offended migraine
    Whenever one said something rude or raised his voice;
Needless to add, she spoke in a ladylike whisper
    Which reached to the back of the class. Hardly my choice
For a stepmother, her motto, Simper Fidelis
    Seemed to please her impatient suitor quite a lot,
Though he would never anticipate by a moment
    The solemnization of the nuptial knot.
Mystified onlooker at the middle-aged antics
    Choreographed in this decorous ritual,
I described them in satiric, copious detail
    On my amorous visits to the hospital.
Whether it was the age or (in my case) the genders
    Of the proper nouns, we found it funny to parse
Declarative sentences that degenerated
    Irresistibly from comedy into farce.
The sex life of adults, or rather men and women,

Was quite unimaginable to me, in spite
Of all the propaganda we were saturated
    In, which failed either to educate or excite.
Indifference proved a critical disadvantage
    In deciphering many a dubious text,
The heroes let alone heroines of most novels
    Appearing to me merely nominally sexed,
However in perverse self-defense I developed
    Generic empathy, the necessary knack
Of instantaneous emotional translation
    Which those in the majority normally lack.
The same literary legerdemain enabled
    Prestidigitators like Proust and Henry James
To produce the desired, desirable illusion
    By means more subtle than simply transposing names.
It was with a similar sense of revelation
    As the first time another boy asked me to dance
That I stumbled upon *The City and the Pillar*
    The first straightforward homosexual romance
I read in English, despite its unhappy ending:
    In such fables the lovers always came to grief,
A fate I found preferable to the betrayal
    Enjoined in such timid tales as *A Folded Leaf.*

On Sundays (but in summer every day is Sunday)
    Fraser courted his superannuated bride
Amid scenery of unparallelled pretension,
    While unwillingly I was taken along for the ride,
Stuck in the back seat, along with the picnic basket,
    And glaring gloomily out at the passing scene,
Magnificent background, insignificant foreground
    Alike often obscured by the shifting rain screen.
Although my father said I might invite Don Wisdom
    To join us, his doctor declared it was too soon;
Furthermore he expressed a facetious reluctance
    To intrude on my father's second honeymoon.
I had to content myself with dropping him postcards
    En route, which hardly original but sincere,
Even while they did not anticipate an answer

Said as clearly as a cliché: "Wish you were here."
The wishful thinking implicit in the subjunctive
      Expressed as sincerely as a mood can express
My conviction that his presence was the condition-
      Contrary-to-fact required for my happiness,
For though the body seems to wander like a planet
      Through the constellations, erratically and far
From its proper centre, the soul remains in orbit
      Round an invisible and stationary star.

To aggravate my misery I was forbidden,
      For my own good, to read in the back of the car
And had nothing to study but the stupid landscape
      Which like a grand technicolour spectacular
Appeared a less fruitful object for contemplation
      Than I imagined more civilized landscapes are.
The ostensible objective of all these outings
      Was the *fête champêtre* or *déjeuner sur l'herbe*,
By which foreign sauce I tried to disguise the come-down
      From my late mother's elaborate and superb
Outdoor banquets. Now a hard-boiled egg and a sandwich
      Were all one was likely to be offered to munch,
Washed down by Adam's ale: a menu reminiscent
      Of that of my usual paper-bag school lunch.
Hence it seemed there were virtues other than domestic
      Which my father required in a prospective bride.
What use these might be in a possible stepmother
      I never discovered; no doubt I never tried.
Fraser's favourite picnic spot, a choice surprising
      In one so level-headed, was the mountainside.
In breath-taking surroundings and dizzy discomfort
      We could partake of the panorama in lieu
Of less elevated but more nourishing rations,
      But I often got indigestion from the view.

Then, less out of tact than boredom, as conversation
      Dried up, insipid, stale and starchy as the food,
Leaving the adults to their dubious amusements
      I slipped away in search of blissful solitude.

The old tag, Numquam minus solus cum quam solus
        Might describe my preferred predicament except
I was not alone, despite father's disapproval
        Of the imaginary company I kept,
Among which that summer a favourite companion
        And guide, The Skeleton Key to Finnegans Wake,
Viewed askance because of the trials of Ulysses,
        Seemed like the ideal vade mecum to take
Along on these lugubrious jollifications.
        One day when we had lunched beside an alpine lake,
A black seemingly bottomless body of water
        Overshadowed by the topless Rockies above,
And exhaling that mysterious melancholy
        The painters of The Group of Seven seemed to love,
I abstracted myself from the family circle
        So that it might be squared, and at loose ends and bored
Wandered along the shore till I came on a dingy
        Which I impulsively pushed off and climbed aboard.
The presence of this skiff is one of those romantic
        Coincidences found infrequently in fact,
Corresponding to the need, or whim, of the moment,
        On which it were folly to hesitate to act.
So clumsily fitting the oars into the oarlocks,
        I began rowing backwards, not at headlong speed,
Seeing I could not face the way that I was headed,
        And watched the wild foreshore foreshorten and recede.
Privacy hard to procure in our cramped apartment
        I rediscovered temporarily afloat;
Shipping oars, I stretched out unmindful of my body,
        Cradled or coffined in the bottom of the boat.
Having found my place in the fable I was reading,
        I let the real world fade, forgotten and remote.
The book that I held like a parasol above me
        Was easier to lie under than understand,
But meanwhile as I riffled through the puzzling pages,
        Switching the enchiridion from hand to hand,
My leaky vessel captured by a sneaky current
        Drifted farther and farther away from dry land.
This I noticed in my horizontal absorption

No more than that I was getting chilly and wet,
Suspending the adventures of H.S. Earwicker
    Barely long enough to light up a cigarette,
While a summer thunder storm brewed also unnoticed
    Overhead among the encircling mountain tops
Till my solitary idyll was interrupted
    By the persistent patter of immense rain drops.

Equally unremarked by me, my frantic father
    And future stepmother, having seen me embark,
Were shouting and waving to attract my attention
    Helplessly from shore, as they watched a squalid, dark
Cloud threatening with squalls about to overtake and
    Overwhelm my unstable, insouciant barque.
It was with annoyance rather than trepidation
    That I sat up and snapped the book shut with a sigh,
Feeling the boat's upsetting irregular motion
    And seeing the waves were getting monstrously high
I abandoned any further attempts at reading,
    An activity discountenanced by the sky.
I could see no future in imitating Shelley,
    Though drowning might seem a poetic way to die.
Nor did I, as one is supposed to in extremis
    See my whole brief life flash before my inner eye,
Rather I thought only of the unfinished poem
    I was working on; which may be the reason why
I find I have completely forgotten the outcome
    Of the catastrophe, except that I survived
Somehow or other, a fact that goes without saying.
    As to the means whereby my rescue was contrived,
I draw a blank. When afterwards I asked my father,
    He, as is his wont with unpleasantness, denied
All memory of the event or that it happened.
    But what would have been his reaction had I died?
Anyhow I made it to shore before the tempest,
    And there another tempest burst about my head:
Why did I sense in their hysterical reproaches
    Indignant disappointment that I was not dead?
An unworthy but not untenable suspicion:

In their relief they certainly seemed to insist
On the irrational risks I ran, and the worry
    I caused by simply continuing to exist.
My father, incensed at having seen me smoking
    In the boat—for he himself had recently quit—
Announced that he was going to stop my allowance,
    "Seeing some of the ways in which you squander it."
I shrugged defiance, but knew I should miss the pittance
    That paid for my pleasures, specifically the fare
Twice a week between New Westminster and Vancouver,
    Which I secretly resolved to obtain elsewhere.
"In future you will have to finance your bad habits,"
    Though he did not say "vices" I knew this implied
Not only tobacco but my hospital visits
    As well as my reading habits, which he decried.
Thus my tacit declaration of independence
    Was elicited by one of those accidents
For which one ought to be everlastingly grateful.
    Freedom is the first fruit of disobedience.

AUGUST: ANY DAY

True to my word, or as good as my resolution
    (If pride did not inspire me, necessity did),
I set out at once in search of gainful employment
    Of the sort available to an unskilled kid:
Mowing lawns, delivering papers, baby-sitting,
    The traditional teen-age occupations that
Befitted my youth and educational status
    As part of the pubescent proletariat.
For most menial tasks I lacked qualifications,
    Like muscles, patience, a lawnmower or a bike,
And nobody we knew had any little children,
    Which, unlike my stepmother, I did not much like.
I tried my hand at anything, but berry-picking
    Was such exhausting stoop labour in the hot sun,
And so unrewarding—I was not nimble-fingered—
    That I quit before the first fruitless day was done.
I answered an ad for a spot as cub reporter
    On the local rag, The New Westminster Gazette,
And was promised the post of High School Correspondent
    When school began; but it was not Labour Day yet.
Was I green enough to believe that journalism
    Had anything more to do with literature
Than digging ditches has to do with architecture
    Or photography with fine art? I am not sure,
But fancy that I saw in part-time occupation
    Something in the nature of an apprenticeship,
And thought that working with words, my favourite playthings,
    Would be at once a training and an ego trip,
Disillusioned soon to find journalistic practice
    The converse of poetic, a linguistic gyp.

The opening I sought in a manner of speaking
    Lay, as often, obviously under my nose,
In the very library where I spent so many
    Hours that might be termed idle but not otiose.

174

Bjorn Daj, sympathetic to my dreams of a token
        Independence, at less than the minimum wage,
Opined that someone of my bookish disposition
    Could hardly do better than to become a page:
It happened the library needed a dog's body
        To shelve books and perform similar simple tasks,
And in short on Daj's and Knight's joint recommendation
        I was hired. If everything comes to him who asks,
How much more to him who is asked, if he is lucky,
        And quick-witted enough to know when to accept.
I had fallen into a marginal profession
        Rather less demanding than rewarding, which kept
Me in pocket money throughout High School and College.
        Wherever there was a library I had hopes
Of casual, not just congenial employment
        However poorly paid, as one who knew the ropes—
Not that these were tricky or difficult to master—
        Brought up in the harem, I learned its ins and outs,
The alphabet and the Dewey Decimal System
        Providing clues to every volume's whereabouts.
In the perfunctory performance of my duties
        Inveterate literacy more than sufficed;
Like a kid in a candy store, I used to sample
        The goodies whereby I was constantly enticed.

Positively the most repugnant of these duties,
        From which I shrank as from a necessary crime,
Keeping an eye on the derelicts in the Reading
        Room, required me to turn them out at closing time.
Till then, each bum must be furnished with reading matter
        Of some kind, whether he wanted to read or not,
Print thus providing a short-term ticket to comfort,
        For the building was kept malodorously hot.
With the design of avoiding such a pathetic
        And smelly end, I put my earnings in the bank,
Apart from what I spent on cigarettes and carfare;
        I had this unfortunate example (which stank)
As much as my father's sententious admonitions
        Or my economical temperament to thank

For my eventual get-away and a life-long
    Addiction to some fairly sordid forms of thrift
As epitomized in the notion of Daylight Saving,
    As if life were an investment and not a gift.

My white-collar job involved some manual labour,
    Like fetching big, bound volumes and putting them back,
But I soon developed the knack of dilatory
    Dawdling in the stacks without quite getting the sack.
Although far from conscientious, I was less lazy
    Than unaccustomed to work; easy to arouse,
My curiosity could not resist the open
    Invitation of my environment to browse.
I dipped into everything I could get my hands on,
    Which was plenty, and masticated not a few
Tasteless treatises and indigestible digests
    In the Kenyon, Hudson or Partisan Review.
To these I began sending my typewritten poems,
    Which were returned with a printed rejection slip,
More than one coming from the eponymous organ
    Of which one day I should wield the editorship.
But foreknowledge would have been feeble consolation
    To a beginner such as I; fourteen years old
And not even, yet, editor of the school paper,
    I would not have believed my future if foretold.
Then one s.a.s.e. came home to roost less bulky
    Than when it was hopefully stamped and self-addressed,
Which turned out to contain a letter of acceptance
    That made me feel as if I had scaled Everest,
Though Bjorn Daj warned me it was no more than a foothill
    And my father true to type remained unimpressed.
I cannot deny this maiden publication
    Went, where both predicted it would, straight to my head;
More and more instead of serving the reading public
    At the library, I stayed in the stacks and read.
This was all right when my protectors were on duty,
    But the other less understanding staff grew vexed:
Being trained to identify books by their bindings,
    I had no business losing mysef in their text.

I wonder why, continually in hot water,
    I was not, for all my inefficiency, fired?
The trouble of finding and training a replacement?
    Perhaps the indulgent interest that had hired
Me in the first place? an influence which diminished
    By half when Miss Knight left without saying goodbye.
In response to my persistent interrogation
    Nobody could, or would, tell me whither, or why.
Uncharitable and, I trust, unfounded rumour
    Described her removal by night to a discreet
Asylum, but I chose to regard her departure
    As a timely, strategic religious retreat.
Yet I detected something obscurely symbolic
    In her sudden exit under cover of night,
As if there were an inherent obscurantism
    In the very name and character of Bea Knight,
As well as the tact and undeniable kindness
    With which she had, so I imagined, timed her flight
To coincide with the long-awaited reunion
    That her presence like an anathema might blight.

Don Wisdom's homecoming, the high-point of the summer,
    An emotional solstice slightly overdue
In August, outweighed in immediate importance
    My first job and even my public debut
In print. No longer need I undertake a journey
    Of an hour each way for the sake of a short talk,
As his parents' house was a block from our apartment,
    A throne's stowaway, only a few minutes' walk—
Not that he ever would again: on that the doctor
    Being prepared to take his Hippocratic oath,
He declared that I should have to do all the walking
    And more than my share of the talking for us both.
Still half paralyzed but considered convalescent
    Because he could hoist himself from wheelchair to bed
And back again by means of his muscular upper
    Torso, his nether limbs a pathetically dead
Weight, he remained nonetheless to his shame dependent
    On others, and plainly resentful of the fact,

Sometimes dismissing my demonstrative devotion,
　　As a drag and deficient in delicate tact.
Tactile values were at the forefront when we wrestled—
　　His idea—mismatched as we were, on the couch,
Which was the closest we ever came to embracing,
　　As I hypocritically squirmed and murmured, "Ouch",
A vain manoeuvre to camouflage my excitement.
　　Then in warm weather he used to take off his shirt,
Displaying the superbly developed equipment
　　In the grip of which he squeezed me so hard it hurt.

His crippled condition insured a certain licence
　　In matters of habit like manners, speech and dress.
His pitiful parents, prematurely permissive
　　Let him do anything he wanted to, unless
Contrary to explicit medical instructions,
　　In practice anything he was capable of,
According to a theory of compensation
　　That confused pity with guilt, indulgence with love.
Furthermore he benefited from the unspoken
　　Assumption that little serious mischief could
Be got up to by anybody in a wheelchair
　　Whom an accident had made unwillingly good.
What matter if he acquired a few minor vices,
　　In view of what involuntary virtue cost?
His folks overlooked his provocative bad manners
　　Without mentioning the full manhood he had lost:
Smoking and drinking, staying up late and bad language,
　　Which in another lad would be accounted crimes,
Were ignored or unhappily tolerated,
　　Though I saw his mother wince in silence at times,
A small, nervous woman one could hardly imagine
　　Producing such an unlikely large, loud-mouthed lad,
Though his heredity was already apparent
　　In the rugged but fleshy good looks of his dad.
The hospital had laid down petty regulations
　　Which the home was helpless to begin to enforce;
Wilfulness anyway was welcomed as a symptom

Of recovery, an expression of life force.
The influence of undesirable companions
  So widely advertised, maligned and dreaded by
Scared parents, was negligible: his sole companion,
  Undesirable or otherwise, remained I.

My once semi-weekly visits becoming daily
  Soon ceased to be visits in the casual way
I was treated and greeted as family, almost
  Unnoticed, a hanger-on or habitué.
My life for the next four years was to be divided
  Unequally among school, my job, and this queer
Attendance, unpaid but not precisely a pleasure,
  On one to whom it nearly sufficed to be near,
As courtiers and the higher orders of angels
  Feel rewarded by proximity to the throne
For tedious, humiliating, thankless service.
  But I marvel, now, that I was ever alone
Long enough to pursue my other, true vocation,
  Not as playmate, punching-bag, pupil, page, or nurse,
But as apprentice in the prolix fabrication
  Of free or at least comparatively cheap verse.
Indifferent to my independent existence,
  Don did not ask what I did when I was not there,
Like the shadow he nick-named me, behind his wheelchair;
  Anyway, he dismissed most poetry as "square",
Understandably, for the unique book of verses
  In his household, Fitzgerald's four-square *Rubaiyat*,
Besides tampering with the genders of the Persian
  Limped in quatrains on feet I even then found flat.
The kind of verse he liked and quoted with enjoyment,
  Oral, or passed from hand to hand in *samizdat*
Or its Canadian counterpart, private printings
  Reproduced in blue or purple mimeograph,
Scatological verses of popular ditties
  And licentious limericks, mostly made him laugh.
Serious literature depressed him, as soppy,
  For it never tickled his funny bone like this.

179

The official authors recommended for study,
    That is, for straight-faced, destructive analysis
Or paraphrase, devoid of discernible humor,
    Only reinforced his deep-seated prejudice.
Then the trouble was that the young expected nothing
    Sanctioned by adults to have any relevance
To their lives and desires and tribal sense of rightness,
    So that few mature masterpieces had a chance
Of acceptance. Today I believe that the process
    Has been reversed, but with debatable success,
Juveniles' supposed preferences being pandered
    To in required reading, as in music and dress.
When we were young, and I say this without complacence,
    The world was old in standards and style, and the young,
While rejoicing in their own borderline subculture,
    Aspired to that world, before the world became young.

Of my own poems, which I showed him with misgivings,
    Don complained that he could make neither head nor tail,
With the infallible smugness of the born critic
    Whose taste can never be faulted when effects fail
To meet with his instantaneous approbation.
    Whatever the cause, it did not strike me as odd
That the object of my veiled verbal adoration
    Should scorn the cult that he had inspired, like a god.
Doubtless Mr. W.H. scanned each new sonnet,
    If he could scan, or read, with something of the same
Uncomprehending but faintly flattered impatience:
    Another sugary conceit from what's-his-name.

At home Don's formal education was continued
    Erratically by means of correspondence school,
Since the handicapped were not accomodated
    In classrooms then. Unmotivated but no fool,
("Unmotivated"—pedagogic talk for lazy,)
    He sometimes called on me, as the more studious,
To help complete his assignments at the last minute,
    Earning between us a respectable B-plus,

A passing mark unquestionably more prestigious
    In that dim, competitive era than today,
When thanks to lax standards and scholastic inflation
    C is a failing grade and half the class gets A.
Although he missed what psychologists call "the social
    Boon of horizontal intercourse with his peers",
I envied Don one chance which he took no advantage
    Of, that of completing several high-chool years
In one, and thus matriculating prematurely;
    But he spent a tenth of the time he would have spent
In school on schoolwork, and treasured his ill-got leisure,
    Or squandered it in dubious divertissement.

The aggressive temper once encouraged in boyhood
    Which found a socially viable outlet less
In academic excellence than in athletics
    Now expressed itself in honeymoon bridge and chess,
Though any game he played could better be termed "cut-throat",
    At the same time he complained that I was no fun
To play with, lacking the instinct of emulation
    And outwardly indifferent as to who won.
Don invariably did, to his unconvincing
    But nonethless vehement affected chagrin:
My role like the devil's, was to put up a struggle
    But never, God forbid, ultimately to win.
Any resemblance to a honeymoon was purely
    Moonshine as far as consummation was concerned;
With the strained intimacy of an ill-matched couple
    We argued and turn and turn about yearned and spurned;
Off the chessboard I was more often checked than mated,
    For which I had his disinclination to thank
More than his disability. I called this stalemate,
    Mimicking his mocking accent *un mariage blanc.*"
Ironically in part the very precondition
    Of the daily proximity I so prized
Would have precluded a closer association;
    Furthermore, he derided desires he despised,
Seldom referring to my earlier avowal

Of affection at the hospital; when he spoke
Of the motives behind my devoted attendance
   He did so obliquely, as an unfunny joke.

Before his return in a wheelchair I had never
   Set foot in the house which would presently become
My second home, but I had loitered on the sidewalk
   Waiting for an invitation that did not come,
In vain trying to picture the inner arrangement
   Of rooms, and in particular which room was his;
But now that I had been admitted as an inmate,
   Everything was different, as it always is.
In the first place, the paraplegic had his bedroom
   On the ground floor, unable to manage the stair:
A windowless walk-in closet next to kitchen
   Became his private retreat, or rather his lair,
Cavernous, crepuscular, untidy and foetid—
   His mother was discouraged from cleaning in there.
The rest of the house, kept meticulously spotless,
   Reflected the values of the blue collar class
For whom anything underhand was damned as "dirty".
   Now it was no longer Don's task to cut the grass
Patch in front as close as his military crew-cut,
   Nor did his mother ever bid him move his feet
So she could dust. His home, larger than our apartment,
   Never seemed quite homelike, because it was so neat.
Out of place amid the ferns and antimacassars,
   The waxed floors and calendar art and bric-a-brac,
The young lay-about on wheels circumambulated
   Or sulked in his stuffy room flat on his back,
Which was of course the only possible position
   For him in repose, save artifically propped
Up, the agility of the aspiring athlete
   Having been untimely and forever short-stopped.
The dark room in which his negative life developed,
   Dominated by an iron hospital bed,
Another uncomfortable, awkward reminder
   That he was as he bitterly put it, half dead,
Revealed itself by bedside lamplight as a muddle

Of sickroom and teenage hideaway, with, amid
Discarded playthings and unfinished airplane models,
    The paraphernalia of the invalid.
And there I used to discover him in the morning,
    Recumbent, carelessly half-covered with a sheet,
Himself a model or a roughly sculptured statue
    Of admirable proportions but incomplete.
Sometimes bored or mortified by his own shortcomings,
    He would not let me in when I knocked at his door,
Till I turned away, fighting back the tears, resolving
    In mortification to trouble him no more,
But often returning later the same day, summoned
    Less by his disingenuous telephone calls
Than by that strong magnetic force that draws the salmon
    Higgledy-piggledy headlong up water falls.

Most North American males (I was an exception)
    Become automotive while still not fully grown,
And even before he obtained a Learner's Permit
    Young Wisdom might be said to have wheels of his own,
For his father had the family Ford outfitted
    For his handicapped favourite with hand controls.
I understood all about the internal combustion engine,
    But could not tell a Studebaker from a Rolls.
Don introduced me to the dreary world of Drive In
    Restaurants and movies, identical everywhere,
Which, whether billed as double shake or double feature,
    Served the same insipid, indigestible fare;
Their main attraction was, they were easy of access,
    As it is said certain unattractive girls are,
But for all his increased mobility Don Wisdom,
    Though he drove o.k., refused to go very far,
As for instance to the rented cottage at Crescent
    Beach to which his parents had offered us the key,
But where he refused to explain his stubborn reluctance
    To spend a weekend alone with the likes of me:
Perhaps I had professed myself only too suspiciously willing
    To wait on him hand and foot? His shyness was such,
In view of his imperfectly functioning body,

That he hated me to see it, let alone touch.
Although my clumsy but sincere offers of service
    Were not motivated by prurience, no doubt
I felt an underhand, private fascination
    With just those things which he was so touchy about.
Thus the modesty that I lovingly remembered
    In circumstances where there was little to hide,
Not only survived the eclipse of the felt object
    But was by shame and frustration intensified,
Suggesting that the principal sexual organ
    (Though everyone thinks he knows better) is the mind:
Don's theoretical interest in such matters
    Had not with his potentiality declined.
'Sex in the head,' deprecated by D.H. Lawrence,
    To any adolescent senselessly bereft
Of all genital capacity and sensation
    Looked like the only possible kind of sex left.
And while most of his red-blooded contemporaries
    In good health seem with a single subject obsessed,
How much more so this young, involuntary virgin
    Whose obsessions could not be physically expressed.
Augustine, another kill-joy, sternly upbraided
    The rebel member for its independent stand,
But Don complained that his had got so independent
    As to be out of touch as well as out of hand,
And notwithstanding an occasional uprising
    Diagnosed as a "spasm" in the hospital,
He was condemned to remain a detached onlooker
    Of a phenomenon he could not feel at all.

Coming of age long before the heyday of Playboy
    And similar educational magazines,
He had somehow amassed an eye-opening treasure
    Trove the like of which I have not seen since my teens:
"The Nubian Slave," and "The Schoolteacher's Confession",
    Oral literature manually reproduced,
Which he used to read aloud while I raptly listened
    As if to the cliff-hanging periods of Proust.
We made of these Arabian Nights' entertainments

Yet another game, where I was challenged to guess
The first word on each page before he would continue,
    A test I performed with predictable success,
The vocabulary and structure of the stories,
    Elementary, hard and fast as formulae,
Mimicking the limits of the human condition
    Like the variations of classical ballet.
Occasionally in their queer cerebral contest
    It was my turn to interpret the doubtful text,
Pausing at the bottom of each page till my partner
    Divined or recalled the beginning of the next.
Nor was this his only pseudosexual outlet.
    He soon began or resumed dating the fair sex,
As he deemed it, though his seemed to me far fairer.
    Whether moved by pity or impressed by his pecs,
Several girls were not averse to his attentions,
    Depending, naturally, on how far they went;
Feminine consensus described him as a dreamboat
    Back before he was capsized in an accident.
Once again, as in the case of my father's courtships,
    I found myself indispensable but *de trop*,
Not as pander but literally as a pusher
    For I wheeled him everywhere he wanted to go
On foot; but when we arrived at our destination,
    Normally the maiden's dwelling, I was dismissed
To another room, as often as not the kitchen,
    While in the living room the couple clipped and kissed.
Thus, exiled, I would read and write and do my homework,
    Or a crossword puzzle if I was truly cross,
Knowing that a third person at a petting party
    Is as welcome as Coleridge's albatross.
Not yet old enough to have discovered the folly
    Of being jealous of a whole gender, I was
Dissatisfied with the nature of the triangle
    While constrained to obey its geometric laws,
But no more unsatisfied than the bumbling lovers
    In the parlour, for whereas two is company,
Until the partnership can be incorporated
    The firm is of limited liability.

Fidgetty after each humiliating visit,
    The lover frequently took it out on the friend
On the way home, while his date pondered the distinction
    Between not going all the way and a dead end.
Yet when in years to come I heard that he had married
    After all, I could not claim to be stupefied;
It would not be the only Canadian marriage
    To preserve the tried virginity of the bride,
Besides he may have in maturity recaptured
    Those masculine faculties blasted in the bud.
Though I knew of his de facto emasculation,
    As it was I always pictured him as a stud
To myself, and this stereotypical daydream
    Contained a *soupçon* of psychological truth,
For the hope that he would somehow someday recover
    Sprung eternal with the resilience of youth—
Hence the clear-eyed despair that sometimes made him cruel,
    When he teased me or pinched me or twisted my arm,
Inflicting myriad verbal humiliations
    Which hurt without doing any visible harm.
Or was it his all too natural irritation
    At my constant presence which he could not elude
Or do without, with its inadvertent reminder
    Of freedom of movement, plus my solicitude?
Did inability to experience pleasure
    Explain this perverse propensity to give pain,
Which every patient recognizes as more ancient
    Than anything, and resignation greets, "Again?"
But which I did not pretend to endure with patience
    At his hands; besides he liked to hear me complain,
Up to a point: he arbitrarily relented
    When he had brought me to the breaking point, afraid
Lest I implement my desperate threats of leaving
    Forever; but needless to say, I always stayed.

It being supposed neither natural nor healthy
    At our age to skulk indoors all day in the dark,
On sunny afternoons our usual excursion
    Led through the sleepy streets and shady Royal Park,

Over the undistinguished bridge that spanned the Fraser
        River, 'outpacing bargain, vocable and prayer',
To the other side where a level nether landscape
        Lay open and accessible to his wheeled chair
In which we had found, to our mutual frustration,
        That we could not by any means go everywhere.
When not restive prisoners of the drippy weather
        In which British Columbia always abounds,
Without access to public places of amusement
        Not only poverty and youth placed out of bounds,
We had to fall back for recreation on nature,
        As without noticing we had been taught to do
All our lives, though Don would no more have quoted Wordsworth
        Than have effusively admired the wide-spread view,
From the bridge, of dirty river and fertile delta,
        Except as an hypothetical habitat,
Often saying he wished he lived on Zulu Island
        Because it appeared so negotiably flat.
The slopes on which his home and mine were situated
        Made it impossible for him to get about
Outside by himself without the cooperation
        Of someone like myself, an amateur mahout
Of the elephantine wheelchair; often our only
        Destination, that adolescent Mecca, Out.

Out we went, then, one warm evening in late August,
        But only so far as I could easily push
Him through the paths of the park to a secret thicket
        Where we stopped or bogged down in the overgrown bush
To smoke our home-rolled cigarettes, a filthy habit
        That had the status of an adult, manly vice,
Side by side in the close, companionable twilight.
        "You know, for a four-eyed fairy you're pretty nice,"
He mumbled, an unprecedented declaration
        That emboldened me to try to give him a hug.
"Knock off the funny stuff!" he gruffly remonstrated,
        Brushing aside my timid embrace with a shrug,
Before countering with an improper proposition
        Which I, though properly shocked, was slow to resist:

That I give a one-sided, first hand demonstration
　　Of those puerile manoeuvres he so sadly missed,
Which performed, would transform our relationship, making
　　Him a voyeur and me an exhibitionist.
This opportunity, couched almost as an order,
　　I was as reluctant to reject as enjoy,
It seemed to me so perverse, selfish and coldblooded,
　　Unlike the reveries of reciprocal joy
I had toyed with in the face of medical hearsay,
　　Psychologically if not morally all wrong,
Yet the nearest thing to physical consummation
　　Our bodies could know, as we had known all along.
My duty and pleasure were to act as his stand-in,
　　Enabling him to feel again at second hand
That simple-minded sensation that he had tasted
　　Too briefly before being in effect unmanned.
I was no more than a manipulated puppet,
　　Twisting and jerking at my master's mute command,
As long ago in the public library basement
　　I had acted out my childish imaginings
By means of hand-puppets, I now myself embodied
　　His wishes as he pulled imaginary strings,
And my embarrassment gave way to satisfaction
　　At the realization I was doing this
For his sake, as an act of love and surrogation—
　　Would that he could have partaken of the brief bliss,
Which he observed, as he produced it, with detachment,
　　Denying me a last minute climactic kiss,
Then rejecting me as if I were self-polluted:
　　"O.K. the show is over now, you can get dressed."
As soon as I had satisfied his scientific
　　But undeniably envious interest
He discarded me till the next so far unscheduled
　　Command performance, like a slack marionette,
And with a few animadversions on my prowess
　　Sat back and lit another hand-made cigarette.

Thus my first intimate encounter with another,
　　For which I had so long and prayerfully prepared,

Came off rather as a curious confrontation,
    Barely mutual in-so-far as hardly shared.
But while the experiment might be inconclusive
    It had proved something, even limited experience
Recognizing the identity of the other
    As more important than all other elements,
Whatever the principal reagent's reaction,
    Even ostensibly studied indifference.
Attached to the wheel that was my reward and torment
    For trying, like Ixion, to embrace a cloud,
I sensed that while the incident might be repeated
    It could never be rehearsed between us aloud.
The society in which we were born-and-bred members
    In however dubious standing doubtless must
Have measured the gravity of matters according
    To the openness with which they were not discussed,
Thus love was accorded much meaningless lip service
    Whereas the tribute of silence was paid to lust,
About which any attempt to be more outspoken
    Was met with frigid, inarticulate disgust,
An attitude that was dumbly exaggerated
    In the case of The Love That Dared Not Speak Its Name,
The rock whereupon our natural frankness foundered
    And sunk beneath speechless waves of culpable shame,
A discretion that may appear somewhat excessive,
    Seeing that our secrets were essentially the same.

Be that as it may, our relationship continued
    Unchanged on a day to day basis for four years
Till one Saturday morning in our eighteenth summer
    When his teasing had once more reduced me to tears
And I slammed out of his house and his life forever,
    Though I did not know as much at the time, at least
Until I left home a few weeks later for college
    And the seductions of the nefarious East.
If at the outset of that already related
    Story I overlooked my farewells to my friend,
It may be in part because I found a beginning
    Infinitely hard to recognize, like the end.

Daryl Hine was born in 1936 in British Columbia, Canada, and read Classics and Philosophy at McGill University, before going, with the aid of the first of several grants, to live in Paris. He came to this country in 1962, and in 1967 took a Ph.D. in Comparative Literature at the University of Chicago, where he has subsequently taught, as well as teaching at Northwestern University and The University of Illinois (Chicago). From 1968 to 1978 he edited *Poetry* magazine. He has published ten collections of verse, including a *Selected Poems* (Atheneum, 1981). Atheneum also published his verse translations of *The Homeric Hymns*, 1972, and *Theocritus: Idylls and Epigrams*, 1982.